*Authentic*

*Blackness*

NEW AMERICANISTS  *A series*

*edited by*

*Donald E.*

*Pease*

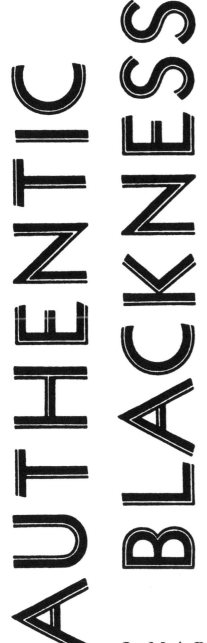

# AUTHENTIC BLACKNESS

The Folk

in the

New Negro

Renaissance

DUKE

UNIVERSITY

PRESS

DURHAM

& LONDON

1999

J. MARTIN FAVOR

© 1999 Duke University Press
All rights reserved
Printed in the United States of America on acid-free paper ∞
Typeset in Carter & Cone Galliard by Tseng Information Systems, Inc.
Library of Congress Cataloging-in-Publication Data appear on the last
printed page of this book.

# Acknowledgments

What is now a book began as a casual discussion. That discussion then progressed through various stages, including seminar paper, dissertation, and draft manuscript. Along that way I have received counsel, aid, and intellectual and emotional support from many generous people and several fine institutions. Although I may leave out some important names, please know that even those people not mentioned are due gratitude and have my sincere appreciation.

I extend deepest thanks to the University of Michigan, the Committee on Institutional Cooperation, Williams College, and Dartmouth College for their financial and institutional support over the life of this project.

Thanks also are due to the many people who have helped me shape the ideas of this project. Among those whose vibrant intellects guided me in the early stages of this work are: Michael Awkward, Alan Wald, Sandra Gunning, Earl Lewis, Rafia Zafar, Lemuel Johnson, and David L. Smith. Cecilia Infante deserves special recognition for believing in this project at moments when even I did not.

My students at Williams College and Dartmouth

College have also played a crucial role in helping and sustaining my endeavor. Their support, insightful comments, and good humor have been more encouragement to me than those outstanding students could have known.

I also wish to acknowledge my friends and colleagues at Dartmouth College who have provided interest, effort, and intellectual sustenance on behalf of the project. In particular, I owe much gratitude to William Cook, Jonathan Crewe, Brenda Silver, Alexander Bontemps, Barbara Will, Victor Walker, Keith Walker, Ray Hall, and Ivy Schweitzer. My friend, colleague, and editor Donald Pease deserves much of the credit for making this book what it has become.

I would also like to thank the editors and staff at Duke University Press, particularly Reynolds Smith, Sharon Parks Torian, Bill Henry, and Amy Ruth Buchanan. Their efforts on my behalf have been truly amazing.

Although it is my name that appears on the cover of this book, the project has been a collaborative effort involving all the people listed above, as well as family and friends too numerous to mention here. I hope that all of you who have touched this project in any way recognize that I could not have done it without you. And I hope that, within these pages, you can find something of value.

# Discourses of Black Identity: The Elements of Authenticity

Who is African American? What defines blackness? These are questions to which we often pose "commonsense" responses. Americans—both black and white—invoke racial categories with regularity. More often than not, we have an intuitive sense of who belongs to what group even if we can't exactly articulate why. If we explore these questions with a little more rigor, however, we begin to see that our notions of racial identity are fraught with complexity, contradiction, and paradox.

F. James Davis's 1991 study *Who Is Black?* offers a historical discussion of how, from colonial times forward, the legal precedent and social custom have helped define blackness along the lines of the "one-drop rule." Yet even (or perhaps especially) the law has been inconsistent about which of us "qualify" as African American. When it comes to attempts to quantify the amount of "black blood" in a person, there is no single standard that defines African American identity in the eyes of the state.

The legal status of blackness, however significant, is no more culturally important than people's everyday lived experience of their own racial identity. A cursory and anecdotal glance at the subject reveals that—even outside the rules and strictures of the law—the definition of blackness is constantly being invented, policed, transgressed, and contested. When hip-hop artists remind themselves and their audiences to "stay black" or "keep it real," they are implicitly suggesting that there is a recognizable, repeatable, and agreed upon thing that we might call black authenticity. By the same token, one can still hear the epithet "Oreo" being tossed at certain people; generally proffered as an insult, it suggests that such a person is black on the outside but white on the inside. The term is intended to question a person's authenticity regardless of phenotype. A dark-skinned person can be "internally white" while a light-skinned person might have all the qualities of "real blackness." Furthermore, the "Oreo" insult implies that the definition of blackness itself has foundations outside physical pigmentation. In common speech, we see that our notions of African American identity rely on complex, though perhaps not thoroughly examined, intersections of attitude, style, tradition and—most important for this study—class, gender, and geography.

Marlon Riggs's documentary film of 1995, *Black Is, Black Ain't*, is one of the latest efforts by African American artists to examine and question this notion of black authenticity. The title of the film itself points to the difficulty of explicitly defining African American identity in any shorthand fashion; it refuses to delineate the boundaries of blackness even as it invokes the category as truly experienced and, indeed, necessary. There is something out there we call (and believe we "know" to be) blackness, even if it is difficult to say exactly what it is. In his efforts to expand our sense of African American identity, Riggs draws comparisons between himself as a gay filmmaker, feminist scholars, Ivy League graduates, and members of the middle class. What they all have in common is that they are phenotypically black; they also share the fact that they suffer what we might call a crisis of authenticity. They have all been accused of being not "truly" African American. That is, sexuality, attitudes toward gender, and class status have somehow rendered their racial status as African Americans less "real." Again, we must push beyond skin color if we are to discuss who is black and how blackness is defined.

Riggs's film takes pains to point out that these crises of authenticity are not merely contemporary phenomena. African American social and intellectual history is replete with examples of the struggle over the definition of black identity and its corollary of authenticity. The perceived necessity to delineate ideologically and aesthetically that which is most "real" about African American experiences has been a driving force behind social and artistic movements. In the discussion that follows, I will focus mainly on the Harlem Renaissance, also known as the New Negro Movement or the New Negro Renaissance. I choose this period between the world wars not because it is either particularly unusual or famous but rather because the artists and intellectuals of the era were especially self-conscious about their (re)construction of African American identity. The very idea of the "New" Negro implies an "Old" Negro who is somehow outdated, inadequate, or insufficient for the new cultural moment; the question of what constitutes blackness has to be rethought and reasserted. A sense of "Renaissance" calls up images not only of the flowering of European culture but also of rebirth, the idea that African American arts and letters must be born anew to reflect the concerns of a new age. Yet even at moments of great cultural achievement, are the redefinitions of racial identity and reconstructions of aesthetics without their discontents? The goal may be more accurately to represent the African American experience, but can there ever be such a thing as *the* African American experience? How did artists and intellectuals of the Harlem Renaissance (or any period) struggle to paint a more representative or authentic portrait of black Americans? Is such an undertaking even possible given the diversity of people one might call African American?

My purpose here is to examine various utterances that go into the formation of the critical discourse of literary blackness, and to demonstrate that while some utterances may indeed provide fruitful means of examining texts, they may also limit the ways in which one can read African American literature. By privileging certain African American identities and voices over others, the critic of African American literature often restricts too severely his or her scope of intellectual inquiry into the construction of racial identity. Further, certain privileged utterances also pose problems for the artist who creates works dealing with the topic of black identity. I submit that many writers feel the necessity of writing themselves into a privileged discourse of black identity, yet some authors, as they engage in a specific discourse of blackness, also undermine a "natural"—or, more precisely, "naturalized"—sense of African American literary identity by asking pointed questions about the underlying ideologies of "race" and engaging in a sometimes playful, sometimes disturbing destabilization of the black subject.

First I shall consider the critical discourse of blackness that places the "folk"—southern, rural, and poor—at its forefront; how and to what ends did such a discourse come into being? How, then, is the artist to deal with, say, a member of the Northern urban middle class whose relation to questions of everything from economics to orature might be substantially different from his or her "folk" counterpart? Moreover, why are certain utterances—especially those emanating from (a construction of) the "folk"—accorded a greater value, a larger measure of "authenticity," than others? Both Houston Baker and Henry Louis Gates Jr. have touched on these issues at some length. Indeed, both scholars have developed theories of African American literature that are highly invested in specific notions of folk identity.

Baker takes a vernacular approach to the study of black literary history. He writes that he desires to demonstrate "*how* black narrative texts written in English preserve and communicate culturally unique meanings" through forms of cultural expression that represent "black" subjects in "black" ways.[1] According to Baker, "Afro-American culture is a complex, reflexive enterprise which finds its proper figuration in blues conceived as matrix."[2] He further describes the blues as "the performance that sings of abysmal poverty and deprivation,"[3] and he goes on to say that "each figuration [of the blues] implies the valorization of vernacular facets of American culture."[4] Baker insists on the antielitist exploration of African American culture; he implies that the best way to understand blackness in America is to scrutinize the lower classes, where, in his view, the most authentic blackness is to be found. Certainly Baker's points are useful in many instances, but does his insistence on a vernacular reading of African American culture and literature neglect some issues of "race" itself? One consequence of Baker's vernacular-centered criticism is to privilege the African American folk and its cultural forms in the discourse of black identity. If the uniqueness of African American culture lies in its folk forms, then the authenticity of folk identity is privileged in the discourse of black identity.[5] This is a powerful model for scholarship, but can it also account for the presence and products of the black middle class? Does this particular vernacular also have room for, say, immigrants from Africa and the Caribbean and the vernaculars they bring along with them?

Baker's groundbreaking formulation also raises another issue with which a number of Harlem Renaissance authors (and, indeed, African American authors of all periods) struggle, namely, the links between color, "race," and culture. Does a person's racial categorization, the classification of the subject as black, white, or other, necessarily lend a "racial" character to that person's cultural work? Further, how accurately may one describe cultural difference in terms of "race"? Although politics of "race" in the United States have indisputably given rise to specific cultural forms, to what extent are those forms in their origins primarily based on color? In their transmission across generations, do they maintain the imprint of one color, or are they not also greatly inflected by factors such as class, geography, and gender? Baker's formulation of the African American vernacular begins to get at many of these questions as it acknowledges "racial" culture as always already inflected by class.

Similarly, Henry Louis Gates Jr. has characterized the task of African American literary critics as the study of "the black vernacular tradition . . . [in order] to isolate the signifying black difference."[6] The implication is that difference lies only in the vernacular, and that vernacular is a language spoken most often by persons of the folk, or those with a conscious connection to folk culture. Describing his own vernacular theory, Gates writes that "signification is a theory of reading that arises from Afro-American culture; learning how to signify is often part of our adolescent education. That it has not been drawn on before as a theory of criticism attests to its sheer familiarity of form."[7] The implications of this statement for the discourse of black identity are profound. Gates invokes the "common" nature of signification as authority for its use in critical theory. Because signifyin(g), in his vision, marks a certain period in the formation of black identity, that cultural practice may take a central position within that discourse. Indeed, his formulation suggests that "we" does not include persons other than African Americans (unless by some circumstance they were raised in African American culture), privileging in the discourse of identity not only the vernacular but a particularly racial construction of it.[8] Here again the intersection of "race" and culture is significantly inflected by class position. Moreover, Gates's use of "often" has significant implications for the links between color and culture; what is the position of those who did not have signification as part of their adolescent education? Are their culture and their identity somehow less "Afro-" because of their distance from the vernacular? Perhaps not, but their voices may often be less privileged within the discourse of black identity. Emphasizing the unique nature of African American literature, isolating the important singularity that allows us to categorize a work as black or African American, is important, progressive work. Yet returning ultimately to folk culture, or some derivation of it, may also prove problematic because such a strategy never quite destabilizes notions of "race" and difference that can be, and have been, used in the service of political and cultural oppression. The concept of the "folk" as a marker of authentic blackness is a valuable means for understanding African American literary history; it may, however, be even more suggestive when viewed as part of a matrix of possible African American subject positions.

It is important to recognize, however, the political and literary significance of Baker's and Gates's particular discourse formation. The privileging of the folk and vernacular is a pointedly political act in a racialist society. By maintaining the primacy of the folk and folk culture, Baker and Gates, among others, offer resistance to crushing assimilationism and/or naturalization of African American cultural inferiority. Their work is not merely an arbitrary intellectual endeavor, but rather a strategic assertion of cultural pride and political power. They consciously invoke the vernacular in a "deformation of mastery," yet that liberating deformation has pitfalls of its own.

Etienne Balibar, writing about cultures that have promoted racist ideologies, has said the following:

> The quest for nationality through race is necessarily doomed, since racial or cultural "purity" is merely the name of this quest, this obsession. Moreover, it always turns out that in actual practice the criteria invested with a "racial" (and a fortiori cultural) meaning are largely criteria of social class; or else they wind up symbolically "selecting" an elite that already happens to be selected by the inequalities of economic and political classes. . . . These effects run directly counter to the nationalist objective, which is not to re-create an elitism, but to found a populism: not to expose the historical and social hetero-

geneity of the "people," but to exhibit their essential unity. . . . the racial-cultural identity of the "true nationals" remains invisible, but it is inferred from (and assured by) its opposite, the alleged, quasi-hallucinatory visibility of the "false nationals." . . . One might as well say that it remains forever uncertain and in danger: that the "false" are *too* visible will never guarantee that the "true" are visible *enough*.[9]

Although Balibar here has in mind cultures based on the exclusion of "minorities"—Jews, blacks, immigrants, colonized native populations—we can learn something from this passage about the quest for authenticity and the construction of race within "minority" discourse itself. Indeed, the dynamics of positing authenticity need not differ wildly between a group bent on racial nationalism for destructive, or even genocidal, purposes—anti-immigrant movements, for example—and a group using notions of authenticity to combat racism itself, for instance, certain forms of black nationalism. They both seek to create unity in the face of an "other," and whereas their notions of what constitutes the "elite" will differ, they are both dependent on them. This is not to say that all forms of nationalism are equally beneficial or detrimental. Without nationalism and its corresponding senses of cultural and communal identity, anticolonialist movements might never win the people's right to self-determination and nondomination. So it is not to condemn nationalism as such that I quote Balibar; rather, I point to his formulation because it points to some instructive and occasionally problematic ways in which we imagine ourselves into particular groups based on cultural and racial difference.

Cornel West has suggested much the same thing as Balibar when, in his book *Race Matters,* he discusses "The Pitfalls of Racial Reasoning." West writes, "Escalating black nationalist sentiments—the notion that America's will to racial justice is weak and therefore black people must close ranks for survival in a hostile country—rests [*sic*] principally upon claims of racial authenticity."[10] West goes on to discuss the controversy surrounding Clarence Thomas and Anita Hill, which publicly raised such questions as " 'Is Thomas really black?' 'Is he black enough to be defended?' 'Is he just black on the outside?' "—all questions that will bear a striking significance for the authors in this study, in terms of both their critical histories and their literary fictions. In attempting to answer those kinds of questions, West astutely reminds us that "blackness has no meaning outside of a system of race-conscious people and practices."[11] Given the ideological, class, and gender implications of the Thomas-Hill controversy, we can begin to see how, long after the Harlem Renaissance, the construction of authentic identity—out of largely non-color-related building blocks—remains an issue of fierce debate. After all, the dark-skinned Thomas's *color* is not at issue. Rather, what is being questioned here is politics, gender, class, and perhaps even Justice Thomas's relationship to some current prevailing notion of the African American folk. That is, is Justice Thomas down with the people in the hood? That West calls the creation of strict notions of authenticity a "pitfall of racial reasoning" demonstrates a need not to reify identity in reaction to oppression but rather to question the assumptions (especially those about purity and difference) that form the foundation of both the oppressor's and the oppressed's identities. Rather than reproducing the system of similarity and difference, we should be seeking to dismantle it.

Let us return to Balibar for a moment, and the implications of his statement for African American literary criticism. Given the privileged position of the folk in African American literary criticism, it would appear that there is, indeed, an elite at least in part "selected by the inequalities of economic and political classes." Of course, with respect to black culture, this is the elite of the folk, those of the southern rural underclasses who have suffered most, those (and note the fascinating linguistic parallel between Balibar and Ralph Ellison) who are most invisible. And while this common ground of second-class status does create a sort of populism, it simultaneously creates rifts and a type of antielitist elitism. Populist elitism facilitates a critique of the black bourgeoisie. E. Franklin Frazier, for instance, criticizes the black middle classes for living in a "world of make-believe" rather than recognizing the second-class status that their blackness, in fact, confers on them. The bourgeoisie may indeed be black, but only "falsely" so in that they insist on maintaining distance from the "more authentic" folk. Historical and social heterogeneity is exposed and becomes a problematic area of contention within the antiracist, antioppressive movement. What also comes to light in such a formulation of folk-cultural identity is a construction of culture as a static entity. It appears as though one leaves "the culture" if one attains a measure of class mobility. But aren't cultures in fact dynamic? Must not we be able to account for ways in which cultural practices transform over time and individuals maintain a relationship to their heritage while simultaneously exploring new territory? Positing too-concrete bonds between authenticity, culture, color, and class risks reliance on a vision of identity so dependent on marginality as its legitimizing feature that it can never effectively deconstruct the center, which, in turn, may hold the margins to be inauthentic. By relying too heavily on a critique launched from the margins, we risk never being able to dismantle those margins without wholly erasing ourselves; in an effort of self-preservation, marginal we must remain. In combating an oppression based on the category "race," we may re-create the notion of "race" itself and, in doing so, hazard laying the framework for a new type of essentialism that potentially reproduces many facets of the old one.

In 1926, at the very height of the Harlem Renaissance or the New Negro Movement, W. E. B. DuBois published in *Crisis* the following series of inquiries in a column entitled "A Questionnaire":

1. When the artist, black or white, portrays Negro characters is he under any obligations or limitations as to the sort of character he will portray?

2. Can any author be criticized for painting the worst or the best characters of a group?

3. Can publishers be criticized for refusing to handle novels that portray Negroes of education and accomplishment, on the grounds that these characters are no different from white folk and therefore not interesting?

4. What are Negroes to do when they are continually painted at their worst and judged by the public as they are painted?

5. Does the situation of the educated Negro in America with its pathos, humiliation, and tragedy call for artistic treatment at least as sincere and sympathetic as "Porgy" received?

6. Is not the continual portrayal of the sordid, foolish, and criminal among Negroes convincing the world that this and this alone is really and essentially Negroid, and preventing white artists from knowing any other types and preventing black artists from daring to paint them?

7. Is there not a real danger that young colored writers will be tempted to follow the popular trend in portraying Negro character

[*sic*] in the underworld rather than seeking to paint the truth about themselves and their own social class?

In 1987, *Black American Literature Forum,* in a two-part series edited by Henry Louis Gates Jr., reprinted DuBois's query.[12] Obviously, even the passage of sixty years has not resolved the question in the African American community as to what constitutes the "proper" portrayal of black Americans. Perhaps the sometimes divisive issue of "proper" representation may never be resolved (and, indeed, why should it be?), but the resolution of those questions is less important than the underlying issue they point out. In posing these questions, DuBois and Gates call attention to what we might call, in the Foucauldian sense of the term, "discourse" — "the general theme of a description that questions the already-said"[13] — the discourse of black identity. DuBois and Gates question a group of concepts about black identity; it is those concepts to which I shall refer as the discourse of black identity. Although "A Questionnaire" does not pretend to lay bare all the subtleties of what it is to be black in the United States, it does try to illuminate some of the basic methods of fictionalizing African American status. These questions in *Crisis* and *BALF* attempt to frame the mode of black characterization during — and by implication, before — the Harlem Renaissance by offering a wide range of possibilities of "proper" portrayal that lay the boundaries of the discourse of black identity.

As DuBois's "Questionnaire" points out, however, long before Baker and Gates, there were theories of African American culture and literary representation that had at their foundation the valorization of some notion of the African American folk. The rift between "true" and "false" folk and bourgeoisie existed, too. Uniqueness lies in difference, and difference is best represented by a particular class stratum. Class becomes a primary marker of racial difference; to be truly different, one must be authentically folk. In what ways, then, does this folkness manifest itself in African American literature? What are the markers of authentic folk identity, or in the case of the bourgeois writer, empathy with the folk; and how did they serve to shape the literary production of the New Negro writer and the Harlem Renaissance period?

Alain Locke writes in his essay "The New Negro" that "if it ever was warrantable to regard and treat the Negro *en masse* it is becoming less possible, more unjust and more ridiculous."[14] Indeed, the call for a

"New Negro" can be seen in itself as an attempt to acknowledge difference within the African American community. Rather than serving as "spokespersons for the race," African American intellectuals, in Locke's vision, were to move forward with a different project. Locke writes that black authors "have now stopped speaking for the Negro—they speak as Negroes."[15] That is, writers should have the leeway to assert their own unique set of circumstances as it relates to their identity rather than adhering to a specific representational protocol. What Locke describes is a shift in the goals of African American literary production, a re-placement of emphasis that signifies difference rather than sameness among African Americans. Black writers, Locke asserts, are beginning to free themselves "from the minstrel tradition and the fowling-nets of dialect" that mark white expectations for black American literature.[16]

If those dehumanizing notions of blackness are swept away, what replaces them in the discourse of African American identity? DuBois suggests that "catholicity of temper . . . is going to enable the artist to have his widest chance for freedom," a freedom that will destroy "racial prejudgement which deliberately distorts Truth and Justice, as far as colored races are concerned."[17] DuBois advocates a wide range of black representations and acknowledges a broad spectrum of black experience while still insisting—at least rhetorically—on the validity and authenticity of African American experience regardless of class. At the same time, however, DuBois' own writing promotes certain types of experience and cultural practice as more central than others to African American art. When DuBois describes "a single phrase of the music in the Southern South" or "that past which . . . in a half shamefaced way we are beginning to be proud of," he is, indeed, suggesting that specific geographies and historical moments (as distinct from, yet intricately interrelated to, class position) are central to the understanding and production of black literature.[18]

An examination of DuBois's seminal *The Souls of Black Folk* makes this nexus of history and geography more abundantly clear. Even as a "Negro of education and refinement," DuBois feels the necessity to travel south to create a more complete notion of his own racial identity. When he proclaims, "How hard a thing is life to the lowly, and yet how human and *real*" (my emphasis), DuBois himself insists that the understanding of a southern, rural folk is the key to gaining a "proper" perspective on black America.[19] Despite his appeal for "catholicity of temper," DuBois places some notion of the folk at the center of the discourse of black identity, and *Souls* is a key text in laying foundations of twentieth-century discussions of African American identity. One need only note DuBois's most unfolk-like background—raised in Great Barrington, Massachusetts, graduate of Harvard, bourgeois intellectual—to see how central the folk is to determining black identity. Indeed, DuBois feels the necessity to write himself into the folk through *Souls* in an effort to prove himself as a legitimate critic and theorizer of black culture and identity. More than a mere intellectual pose for the sake of critical modishness, DuBois's move reveals the ability, perhaps even the necessity, of the African American to perform various aspects of his or her racial being. Certainly the demographics of the African American population at the turn of the century—with the majority of black people living in the rural South—would strongly suggest that one should make it a point to study the rural folk if one is to understand African American culture. My point, however, is that a majority does not necessarily create an exclusive authenticity. Part of what I find most fascinating about DuBois is that he willingly submerges aspects of his status as "a brilliant Yankee Negro from Harvard and Europe" in an effort to draw on—indeed, to make central to his arguments about culture—the African American folk tradition.[20] In a series of conscious moves, DuBois writes himself into a folk positionality that lends authority to his explication of blackness in America. Yet "race" must be, at least in some respects, performative rather than essential to make such a transformation possible.

Whereas DuBois's sentiments predate the Harlem Renaissance, Alain Locke embraces many of the same ideas about the "reality" of the southern folk class. At the same time as he touts the diversity of black American experience, Locke extols "those nascent centers of folk-expression" and "the migrating peasant. . . . In a real sense it is the rank and file who are leading, and the leaders who are following."[21] The rural folk, who are in the process of becoming urban proletariat, are the basis of African American experience. To know black culture, the artist or critic must know the folk; folk experience forms the core of the New Negro's identity.

To be sure, this insistence on the centrality of folk (sometimes more precisely expressed as "lower-class") consciousness has endured. Hazel Carby makes this point when she asserts that "our ideas of an Afro-American literary tradition are dominated by an ideology of the 'folk' from fictional representations of sharecroppers";[22] that is, southern, rural, and poor. And in her response to the *Crisis/BALF* questionnaire, Barbara Smith provides an instructive response to the query about the educated African American:

> What concerns me during this era is that being an educated Black person often means being a Black person with little or no racial consciousness whose major preoccupation is with making money and acquiring things. Unless it is a pointed satire, we do not particularly need novels about Buppies.[23]

Although Smith's comments are rooted in contemporary Afro-America, they do recall E. Franklin Frazier's pronouncements of a more sweepingly historical nature. Frazier noted that "the standards of consumption . . . have become the measure of success among the black middle class."[24] Further, Franklin claims that the lives of the black bourgeoisie generally lack "both content and significance."[25] Both Smith and Frazier equate the black bourgeoisie with materialism and a loss of race consciousness. The desire for wealth, it seems, often makes one "less black," or at least a less authentic representative of racial identity. Separated in terms of class from these critics' notions of folk, the black middle class cannot express the "authentic" African American experience. And though most critics are, by definition, middle-class, they work themselves into a strategic alliance with folk privilege by consciously emphasizing aspects of heritage and experience that link them to the folk while downplaying their own similarities to "buppies." Black identity, as formulated on the class basis, requires a certain quotient of oppression; second-class status is essential to racial identity. The normative conditions of blackness derive from second-class status.

Arthur Schomburg begins his essay "The Negro Digs Up His Past" with the telling sentences "The American Negro must remake his past in order to make his future. . . . For him a group tradition must supply compensation for persecution, and pride of race the antidote for prejudice."[26] Whether prejudice can be overcome by race pride is debatable, but it is important to note where Schomburg locates the starting point of New Negro history. "Remake the past" and a "group tradition" point to a history of the masses emanating from slavery and a collective African heritage.[27] Given the task and the circumstances, Schomburg suggests an approach that will remake the hardships of slavery and the study of the people of an entire continent into the focal point of African American cultural production. Of course, such a project will rest on a folk culture from which the vast majority of African Americans come. Although Schomburg also appeals for a breakdown of barriers between black bourgeoisie and folk, saying, "by virtue of their being regarded as something 'exceptional' . . . Negroes of attainment and genius have been unfairly disassociated from the group,"[28] he still desires "that the full story of human collaboration and interdependence . . . be told and realized."[29] To take an exceptionalist view of history could hinder antiracism generally. By viewing black achievement in terms of exception, as the work of a minority faction, the vast majority of the racial group may still be held in second-class status; exceptionalism implies the untalented 90 percent. Refocusing identity on the folk is designed to avoid such pitfalls.

This "rise" of the folk then represents a significant moment in African American literary history and the discourse of black identity. Wilson J. Moses has suggested that we need to reevaluate our notions of which writers constitute the black American canon because "the legitimate roots of black culture are not confined to plantation folklore, the blues style and proletarian iconoclasm."[30] He goes on to proclaim that a folk interpretation—what he calls the proletarian-bohemian interpretation—of black art "has been granted a sort of moral superiority over any other framework of analysis in black literary and intellectual history. This has led to a distorted perception of the 'New Negro Movement.'"[31] Moses demonstrates that racial authenticity is indeed highly class based. I contend, however, that one cannot view racial authenticity as an either-or proposition; writers continually struggle to negotiate the folk-bourgeoisie boundary in an effort to produce art that demonstrates the complexity of "race" as a marker of identity. Notions of folk and bourgeoisie are continually reformed and deformed with an eye toward political gain and artistic achievement. Still, we need to look at the characteristics that critics and authors have identified as "essentially" folk if we are to understand the ways in which those characteristics are manipulated in the construction of race. In seeking out authentic representations of blackness and the uniqueness of black culture, artists had to return to their "origins." Nathan Huggins has suggested that "culture to the educated American had nothing to do with folk roots";[32] the elite of all races had been alienated from their past through an education in classical European civilization. Huggins states further that "the line back to the past was snarled where enslavement and migration from Africa had begun to make the racial past hazy, distant and impossible to know."[33] In an effort to recover that "racial" past, the writer must, to echo Baker's title, journey back to his or her origins. Ultimately, that would mean Africa as the source of racial identity, but the first stop in the United States would have to be the South.

Nicholas Lemann writes, "During the first half of the twentieth century, it was at least possible to think of race as a Southern issue."[34] Lemann's statement is provocative, but not unproblematic; the North was not a racial paradise of unqualified equality or, at minimum, relatively tension-free coexistence. Indeed, whereas European ethnics were for the most part eventually able to "become" white, northern African Americans, wearing the mark of their difference on their bodies, could not shed their racial categorization. Yet with the vast majority of African Americans either residing in, or recently migrated from, the South, "race" could be seen to have a distinct geographic cast in the 1920s. To understand the essence of the black experience, one needed to turn to the South and its figurations of black and white. Among others, Baker has noted the significance of geography in determining the authenticity of race; he describes DuBois's journey in *The Souls of Black Folk,* a journey of a northerner to the South, as "giv[ing] life to a sign ('folk') that connotes a pretechnological but nonetheless vital stage of human development towards ideals of CULTURE. A FOLK is always, out of the very necessities of definition, possessed of a guiding or tutelary spirit."[35] Certainly, Baker's language echoes Locke's of more than a half century earlier. It is in the South that DuBois and other writers and thinkers can find the "spirit" that underlies and best describes the black experience in the United States. "Go South, young intellectual, and discover the true meaning of blackness" becomes a motto of the day.

But merely being in the South is not enough. Racial authenticity lies in even more specific terms. In a period before the urbanization of the black masses, authenticity was also to be found in rural settings. Bernard Bell writes that "the frustrations of coping with an alien urban environment and industrial society encouraged many transplanted black Southerners to cling tenaciously to their folk roots. . . . Race conscious intellectuals and writers began to tap the roots of their ethnic heritage."[36] The movement of a southern rural folk to the urban North (as well as subsequent, though sometimes overlooked, migrations of many of the folk back to the South) contributes to a specific notion of racial authenticity. To maintain a stable identity, migrants turned toward the geography and demography of a racial past; writers seized on this and used it to help define the essential condition of a race. Huggins states that Zora Neale Hurston "used the common, rural Negro" to create a "general assessment of common Negro character and life."[37] Hurston helped to solidify a notion of racial authenticity in southern rural geographies, and if one reads her work as privileging of the folk, it represents a significant gesture in the history of African American literary representation.[38]

Along with southern, rural settings, I feel the need to reemphasize that literary authenticity also lies in class distinctions. When David Levering Lewis suggests that some of Jessie Fauset's middle-class characters are "aristocratically farfetched or celestially elevated, but they are, nonetheless, authentic and saved from caricature because they reflect faithfully the attitudes of a class that was itself a caricature,"[39] he is not legitimizing a representation of the black bourgeoisie as "true blackness." Rather, the authenticity he describes derives from "inauthenticity": class status outside the working classes disqualifies one from racial authenticity.[40] To represent the black middle class is to represent a group in the process of trying to inauthenticate itself, to distance itself from its "true" racial heritage. With the dawn of a more "formal" New Negro Movement, Lewis states that art still adhered to racial conventions that undermined its radical political possibilities. Lewis criticizes Locke, who despite his own valorization of the folk wanted African American art to be "highly polished stuff, preferably about highly polished people, but certainly untainted by racial stereotypes or embarrassing vulgarity. Too much *blackness,* too much streetgeist or folklore—nitty-gritty music, prose, and verse—were not welcome" (my emphasis).[41] For Lewis, the failing of the New Negro Movement is one of continuing to shun the masses of the folk, where the most instructive exegeses of the African American condition lay. Squeamishness about the folk leads to a continued distance from black authenticity.

These masses, however, while united by class-based blackness, are differentiated by gender. And while gender is, of the factors I have listed, the least consistently used category in establishing a concept of folk identity, it is also one of the most complex.[42] In terms of the Harlem Renaissance, it might prove most useful to begin with an assertion by Huggins on the role of gender in depicting the folk. He writes that primitivism "is especially a male fantasy. It is easier to imagine men as roustabouts, vagabonds, bums, and heroes, harder to draw sympathetic females whose whole existence is their bodies and instinct."[43] Although "primitivism" and "folk identity" are not synonymous, they do share similar resonances. It is in a folk culture that denies "the artifices of civility" that African American intellectuals "could see their own lives as being more natural and immediate than" those of whites.[44] Huggins's language points out the liberating possibilities of a "folk primitivism" with distinct class over-tones (vagabonds, bums, etc.), but at the same time, he denies these pos-sibilities to women, suggesting that "perhaps women, whose freedom has natural limitations—they have babies—are essentially conservative."[45] In implying that gender strongly influences at least some constructions of authentic blackness, Huggins widens the scope of the debate over African American identity. The female body becomes a site over which notions of authentic identity and political orientation can be contested.

Further, Huggins's statement points to the ways in which both mascu-linity and femininity might be constructed in conjunction with blackness and whiteness. Both race and gender can bear their outward signs on the body, and a number of authors and critics find themselves in a dilemma when attempting to represent and explicate relationships among "the dif-ferent." Huggins opts to equate the masculine with the cultural and the feminine with the physical, yet that (cultural) blackness, that signifying difference, he describes can be a physical trait as much as sex difference. What I hope to explore in even more detail are the ways in which some Harlem Renaissance authors define—either explicitly or implicitly—the body as the locus of both racial and gender difference and the ways in which the complex figurations of that difference have a profound impact on notions of authentic identity and cultural form. Johnson, Toomer, Larsen, and Schuyler all want to question the ways in which the black (or mixed-race) body serves as the site of a natural or naturalized cultural identity, yet their thinking about the body as being *both* racialized *and* gendered leads them in different directions.

John L. Hodge observes, "An individual's relation to oppression is typi-cally very complex, since an individual may belong, simultaneously, to both oppressed and oppressor groups."[46] Certainly the African American folk male also falls into this category; he can construct his masculinity to give himself a measure of control of feminine blackness. As Cheryl Wall points out: "Women were, of course, historically denied participation in many of these traditions [which help mark authentic African American identity]; for instance, speechifying, whether in the pulpit or on the block, has mainly been a male prerogative."[47] The form of folk expression is gendered by exclusion, meaning that when we speak of folk culture, we generally speak of *male* folk culture. Of course, such a construction leaves out the contributions of African American women to black culture, but that does not mean that those contributions were minor or nonexistent. Indeed, Wall's observation may not be all that accurate, either in terms of religious history or in terms of the explicit connection of the folk with masculinity. It is significant, however, in that it points toward how we need to examine more closely the way gender is manipulated to arrive at a notion of authenticity: how it is portrayed, controlled, embraced, and ignored by both male and female authors. If gender is often sublimated into the concepts of race and class, can we, in the words of Valerie Smith, discover a method of criticism that "holding in the balance the three variables of race, gender, and class . . . destabiliz[es] the centrality of any one"?[48] Or at least we need to look at the ways in which gender, class, and race are invoked to lend authority to particular artistic and critical positions. In the discourse of black identity, gender is employed in various ways, and its influence on the defining vernacular voice is, as I hope to show, nearly always a matter of contention with African American texts.

What, then, is the value of reinventing, challenging, or reconfiguring a category such as "race" and its discourse? Lucius Outlaw has written that "heightened group (and individual) 'racial' identification [has become] the basis for political mobilization and organization without the constraining effects of the once dominant paradigm of 'ethnicity,' in which differences are seen as a function of sociology and culture rather than biology."[49] Indeed, this may seem regressive; in trying to overcome notions of inherent biological inferiority, many have reconstructed "race" as fundamental difference so as to hinder the ease with which distinct cultural practices can be assimilated into (or out of) mainstream U.S. culture. Race is reinvoked as a term of "ultimate, irreducible difference"[50] to avoid the assimilationist tendencies of "ethnicity" criticism. Race becomes a way of insisting on the merits of difference rather than acquiescing to all dominant aesthetic and topical concerns. The concept of basic racial difference counters such critical pronouncements as "In America, casting oneself as an outsider may in fact be considered a dominant cultural trait."[51] Although American authors may cast themselves as outsiders, some are further outside than others; by insisting on the priority of specifically "racial" difference, authors and critics make a significant distinction between American writing in general and writing in America that evolves out of specific historical and cultural circumstances. Reconstructing "race" helps preserve cultural diversity rather than dismissing its importance, although as I have already intimated, certain reconstructions of "race" may also work to reify marginality while simultaneously having positive political and cultural impact.

We are still left, however, with the problem of racial authenticity. Although politically useful, perhaps even necessary, is it doomed, as Balibar might suggest, to catch itself in its own trap? Seeking to give voice to difference, the discourse of black identity relegates competing voices to an obscure and inauthentic position. Does an insistence on African American authenticity to expose cultural uniqueness eventually wind up erasing difference? Is there a point at which the process of differentiation begins to collapse on itself?

These questions about authentic, fundamental difference have been explored in some detail by several feminist and queer theorists, and I shall draw on their work here to see what sort of resonances it has for African American literature and criticism. Judith Butler writes:

> This question of being a woman is more difficult than it perhaps originally appeared, for we refer not only to women as a social category but also as a felt sense of self, a culturally conditioned or constructed subjective identity. The descriptions of women's oppression, their historical situation or cultural perspective has seemed, to some, to require that women themselves will not only recognize the rightness of feminist claims made in their behalf, but that, together, they will discover a common identity. . . . But does feminist theory need to rely on what it is fundamentally or distinctively to be a "woman"?[52]

Butler's question is a good one. The purpose of much oppositional criticism is not merely to counteract prejudices but also to establish a common identity. How far, though, do all those commonalities extend among members of a group? To be "fundamentally or distinctively" one thing or another necessarily requires the elision of internal difference, and the elision of difference is what, in this case, feminism is designed to overcome. Susan Bordo has explored this dilemma and concluded that "to describe the difference gender makes, gender theorists (along with those who have attempted to speak for a 'black experience' uninflected by gender or class) often glossed over other dimensions of social identity and location, dimensions which, when considered, cast doubt on proposed gender (or racial) considerations."[53] Notions of authentic difference may be useful, but they are flawed. They require a reconstruction of gender or "race" that mirrors in its exclusivity of their definitions the kind of essentialism they were originally intended to overcome. What we shall see in the following chapters of this book are some of the ways in which African American writers seek to challenge virtually *all* notions of reified black identity. Their attacks on authenticity attempt to cast doubt on the discourse(s) of racial difference and theorize alternative structures of cultural, national, and personal identity (often based on some idea of coalition across difference) that offer a more liberating potential than the reconstruction of essentialism.

I want to keep in mind, however, Lucius Outlaw's significant observation: "That 'race' is without a scientific basis in biological terms does *not* mean, thereby, that it is without any social value."[54] "Race," whether advanced from a racist or antiracist point of view, is still a powerful category in shaping thought. Ideas about race cannot be dismissed merely because they tend toward the essential; rather, we must investigate the uses, purposes, and consequences of such essentialism. Gates insists that "race is the ultimate trope of difference because it is so very arbitrary in its application. The biological criteria used to determine 'difference' in terms of sex simply do not hold when applied to 'race.' Yet we carelessly use language in such a way as to *will* this sense of *natural* difference into our formulations."[55] Although I contend that the invocation of race is as often deliberate as it is careless, Gates's observation is valuable. We construct "natural" difference through language, and above all, we use that construction in such varied ways at such varied times that it becomes difficult to understand what precisely we mean by it. "Race" is a highly negotiable, very malleable concept; one may formulate it as authentic or nonexistent. However one talks about race, though, it is still there, and it is this interplay between competing constructions that gives "race" much of its significance. My aim is to call attention to competing notions of "race" in the Harlem Renaissance discourse of black identity and to demonstrate the ways in which several African American authors have attempted to stake new territory in the formulation of authentically black subjectivity and positionality.

If class, gender, and geography mark racial authenticity, we can see quite easily how these signifiers of blackness are also exclusive; the middle class—or at least the nonfolk—are excluded from what is "fundamentally or distinctly" African American, as are blacks from geographies other than the rural South and women excluded from specific cultural practices. The borders have been set up in Balibar's sense: the northern urban bourgeoisie, gendered in specific ways, provides a challenge to the "essential unity" of African American people. Evolving out of this distinction is the important issue of how and why "race" becomes a contested notion within the African American community itself. Who may identify with blackness, to what extent, and to what ends?

Within feminist studies, Butler has spoken of

> the illusion of an interior and organizing gender core, an illusion discursively maintained for the purposes of the regulation of sexuality. . . . The displacement of a political and discursive origin of gender identity onto a psychological "core" precludes an analysis of the political constitution of the gendered subject and its fabricated notions about the ineffable inferiority of its sex or true identity.[56]

The naturalization and essentialization of gender marks identity politics. Gender identity is dependent on various influences for its formation, and relying on a concept of the "fundamentally" female or male saps the idea of gender of some of its power to signify difference. By acknowledging the individual's ability to break from normative or authentic formulations of gender, Butler demonstrates that gender is as much performative as it is essential. By playing on and with discursive codes that traditionally indicate gender, a person may embrace at different times different gender identities in the process of achieving different ends. Understanding performance becomes central to understanding identity.

Along similar lines, Baker points out that race may also be "performed," not merely in the traditions of blackface and minstrelsy, but in the effort to praise and validate particular aspects of African American culture. Baker writes that in *The Souls of Black Folk,* "DuBois polyphonically . . . dances before our eyes the drama of RACE in the modern world. His performance is dioramic; it offers a bright, sounding spiritual display of men, women, institutions, doctrines, debates, follies, tragedies, hopes, expectations, and policies that combine to form a 'problem.'"[57] It appears that in the production of his text, DuBois acts out myriad possibilities of black subjectivity. He performs a version of authenticity by making certain choices about class, geography, and gender in *Souls.* DuBois's choices in, and performances of, form(s) are significant enough to influence notions of racial identity. They carry enough weight to give his readers insight into the African American "soul."

The ability to control aspects of African American identity assumes primary importance both for the performers and for those who study the discourse of identity. Those who can bend class and geographic position to their own purposes have the power to shape what "race" is. By reshaping race, they add to the complexity of the discourse of black identity rather than impoverishing it with "false" notions. Of greatest import is the recognition that the control over, or performance of, certain aspects of racial identity points out the nonessential nature of racial categories. As Joel Williamson has suggested about several Harlem Renaissance authors, the focus of their fiction develops into the question "not of whether to be or not to be . . . but of how to be" African American.[58] What it takes in terms of political sentiment, behavior, and considerations of class, geography, and gender to embrace a black identity infused with pride cannot be determined simply by characterizing the African American folk and using that analysis as a basis for literary evaluation. African American artists outside the folk-vernacular tradition have marvelously complex views on racial identity that need to be studied by anyone—racial constructionist or essentialist—who takes a serious interest in how "race" functions in American culture.

In evaluating these considerations, I would like to keep in mind Baker's assertion that "black writers, one might say, are always on *display,* writing a black renaissance and righting a Western Renaissance."[59] What will be of major significance is how those writers choose to display themselves. In writing a black renaissance, how do they go about writing blackness: what choices do they make and why? Also, in what senses are they involved in "righting" the black renaissance as well as the Western one? How do they critique and mold black literary history through their own contributions of fiction? Making choices of form, rhetoric, and content in performing certain aspects of racial identity, what are they pointing out as the most significant consequences of embracing racial identity at all?

The following chapters will focus on texts by "New Negro" authors who have, at best, an ambivalent relationship toward the African American folk and folk culture. Each chapter will concentrate primarily on one aspect of the discourse of black identity in an effort to explicate more precisely the ways in which blackness can, to various ends, be constructed, deconstructed, and reconstructed. An emphasis on one aspect is not meant to preclude the others; for example, that I seize on James Weldon Johnson's dynamics of class status does not imply that gender and geography are superfluous to his construction of race. On the contrary, these factors often work in concert with one another. In the interest of clarity, however, I want to focus on discrete issues in discrete texts.

On a broader level, I hope that in working through these authors' relationships with the "authentically" black, I can point to some ways in which they have invested themselves in questioning the bonds between color, "race," and culture. Although at times they may posit or reaffirm a type of authentic identity, they often do so with an eye toward undermining that very concept. As they develop multiple, competing, and simultaneous African American subject positions in their texts, they offer both an aesthetic and political commentary on the value of "race" as a stable marker of identity, culture, and a field of intellectual inquiry. Moreover, these authors begin to denaturalize a connection between "blackness" and "race"; they see that whiteness is not a nonracial normative condition but a highly constructed concept, another "race" that is often dependent on blackness for its very existence. That is, in interrogating forms of African American authenticity, Johnson, Toomer, Larsen, and Schuyler work toward a critique of whiteness as an "authentic," unproblematic, and central marker of "American" identity and American literary discourse. In doing so, they not only reaffirm the complexity of art and thought in the Harlem Renaissance but also suggest a number of profound theoretical implications for contemporary antiracist art, politics, and pedagogy.

# 2

For a Mess
of Pottage:
James Weldon
Johnson's
Ex-Colored Man
as (In)authentic
Man

James Weldon Johnson's *The Autobiography of an Ex-Colored Man* is an intriguing work if for no other reason than its title. The term "ex-colored" raises issues at the heart of the discourse of blackness: what are the criteria for being "colored," and how does one manipulate them so as to become "ex-colored"? The title implies agency, conjuring images of a divorce sought and received (ex-spouse) or military service departed (ex-marine). Indeed, at its core, the novel interrogates the validity of linking identity to notions of race, and it probes the question of to what ends racial identity should be employed. With *Ex-Colored Man,* Johnson sets up and foregrounds several crucial debates about the way "race" was constructed in the early years of the twentieth century and, indeed, is still constructed today. Johnson observed the ways in which geography and gender contribute to our notions of racial identity, but his most cogent insights come in explaining the relationship of class to race.

*Ex-Colored Man* was originally published in 1912 but was reissued in the midst of the Harlem Renaissance (1927) to much greater acclaim than its initial publication; it is partially on that basis that I include it in a study of texts more strictly "renaissance" in their traditional periodizations. Robert Fleming notes that the 1927 reprint "brought the novel a much larger, and in some cases a more perceptive, audience than did its first publication."[1] It would seem that Johnson's discourse of race struck a chord with a Harlem Renaissance audience already engaged in the cultural work of determining what "blackness" is, though one should not discount the fact that the 1927 edition was also published with Johnson's name attached rather than anonymously as with the 1912 edition.

In placing *Ex-Colored Man* within the Harlem Renaissance, one must also recognize Johnson's position as a "race leader" and leading African American intellectual during the first three decades of this century. Johnson helped mold the course of thought and inquiry within the African American community in several ways. Most important for this study, Johnson had a hand in shaping the aesthetic concerns of the Harlem Renaissance. Bernard Bell states that *Ex-Colored Man* "moves beyond social realism to a psychological explanation of how color and class prejudices alienate the mulatto artist as individual from the darker, poorer members of his ethnic community and warp the natural impulse to affirm his worth and identity as a black American."[2] If, as Bell claims, Johnson's novel marks a new direction in African American fiction, we need to focus even more closely on what the implications of that direction are. Note Bell's own language in describing Johnson's novel: "class prejudices," "alienate," "darker, poorer," "natural impulse," and "affirm his worth and identity." All these phrases mark, in some way, a discourse of black identity that stretches from at least 1912 to the present. Class, often associated with skin color, becomes a distinguishing feature of blackness; there is a "natural" unity of all African Americans, but that unity can be achieved only through the invocation of a discourse that sifts the "truly black" from that which is alienated from blackness.

Several critics have pointed to Johnson's impact on Harlem Renaissance politics and culture with respect to his activities during the first two decades of the century. Stephen Bronz writes that *Ex-Colored Man* is "an extraordinary book that signalled the emergence of the New Negro."[3] Moreover, Judith Berzon includes *The Autobiography of an Ex-Colored*

*Man* along with Nella Larsen's *Quicksand* and *Passing*, Walter White's *Flight*, and Claude McKay's "Near-White" in a listing of Harlem Renaissance works that deal with the theme of "passing."[4] At the same time, Berzon further strengthens the argument for including *Ex-Colored Man* in a study of the Harlem Renaissance by asserting that "the unhappy passer of the middle-class mulatto who denies his or her people is essentially a Harlem Renaissance phenomenon."[5] It is not my intention here to treat *Ex-Colored Man* simply as a "novel of passing"; to do so would be to restrict the range of issues Johnson raises within his text. I do, however, wish to emphasize the links between class status (middle-class) and racial identity ("his or her people," in the sense that these characters *belong* more to one specific racial group than to another) that Berzon foregrounds in her argument.[6] Looking at *The Autobiography of an Ex-Colored Man* as a text concerned with the complexity of racial identity, I plan to demonstrate the enduring nature of the novel's concerns. Further, I hope to point out the ways in which Johnson construes "race" as a performance and goes on to investigate the consequences of this destabilized conception of "race" for the novel's narrator.

As a member of DuBois's Talented Tenth, Johnson was acutely aware of how his cultural position and literary pronouncements would shape African American culture before, during, and after the Harlem Renaissance. Eugene Levy writes that early in his career, "Johnson took as his theme the idea that great men produce a great race."[7] Johnson himself notes that when he graduated from Atlanta University in 1894, he "wanted to get out and do something" for African Americans and consequently turned down a scholarship to Harvard Medical School to become principal of a black school.[8] Although not part of the folk himself, Johnson saw an opportunity to work with the folk, who were "the basic material for race building."[9] As the quotation suggests, even early in his career, Johnson believed that his role was not only to meet and learn about the folk but also to shape them into a vision that he, as an educated African American, had developed. Similarly, in aesthetics, Johnson argued that "the world does not know a people is great until that people produces a great literature and art."[10] Johnson then took the role of the artist, the great man who can represent—at least in part—the talents of the people; tellingly, his *American Negro Poetry* (1922) dedicates twenty pages to eight of his own poems. Only Claude McKay has more poems in the volume, though in a space of only eighteen pages. Consciously writing from a position within the Talented Tenth, what did Johnson view as the benefits and pitfalls of African American racial identification, and what did he think to be the reality of African American identity and the experience that informs it?

Given his own racial, class, and geographic background, Johnson was well aware of the way African American identity had become irreducible to a simple set of criteria by the time he published *Ex-Colored Man*. He realized that African Americans could not be regarded simply as an undifferentiated bloc of persons; he recognized differences within the African American community, particularly "a rising middle class which since emancipation had gradually become differentiated from the Negro masses . . . [and was] deeply imbued with the goals and ideals inherent in the traditional notion of the American dream."[11] Class difference created a rift; there were "the elite" and "the masses," yet these distinct groups were both "black" in the sense that neither enjoyed first-class American citizenship. It was a reaction to white racism that helped move Johnson toward a desire to bridge the gap between elite and mass. As a nascent "race man," Johnson, then, begins to exhibit the condition that bell hooks might call "loving blackness." That is, he takes the first steps toward engaging in an "oppositional black culture that emerged in the context of apartheid and segregation [and] has been one of the few locations that has provided a space" for a positive African American self-image.[12] As we shall see later in this chapter, however, the narrator of *Ex-Colored Man*—unlike Johnson—is more ambivalent in his love of blackness as he comes to recognize that such a position is "so threatening, so serious a breach in the fabric of the social order, that death is the punishment."[13] Indeed, I would suggest that the narrator's ambivalence, embodied so eloquently in the novel's final paragraph, arises from a deep understanding of precisely how racial categories (both blackness and whiteness) are constructed, learned, and socially reinforced. He can never be quite sure if that which he feels he should love is authentically, tangibly there.

Johnson himself has some similar moments of recognition in his own biography, though with significantly different results. As a college student in the South, a geography that recalls DuBois's education at Fisk and the education of many African Americans at historically black universities in the South, Johnson writes that he "began to get an insight into the ramifications of race prejudice and an understanding of the American race problem. . . . I received my initiation into the arcana of 'race.'"[14] He comes to feel discrimination undifferentiated by class, yet it is a condition he must *learn*. Two implications of this are particularly striking. The first is that Johnson consciously sets out to learn about a black condition marked by racism, one for which his own cultural background had not prepared him. That is not to say that Johnson himself had never been exposed to racism, but that he located the most pernicious effects of this kind of bigotry outside of his own early experience and explicitly foregrounds that condition. Second, although racism is a quotidian and visceral problem, Johnson, though active as a political and community leader, also attacks it by posing an aesthetic and artistic challenge, demonstrating a belief that racism must be undone through representation as well as through more direct political activism. Indeed, as we shall see later, he comes near suggesting that racism is precisely a misleading, inaccurate type of representation.

At the same time, however, Johnson was a "race man" who was devoted "to attempting to raise the status of his black brothers."[15] And although "race men" may have been, at this point in African American history, largely mulatto, their goal was to improve the standing of black Americans regardless of color differences. Indeed, Joel Williamson has written that "in their labors for the race there seemed to be little color exclusiveness among the mulatto elite."[16] That is, despite pigmentation, the elite sought political and cultural advancement for a broadly inclusive idea of African Americans. In poetics, this took the form of advocating types of African American representation that would "be capable of voicing the deepest and highest emotions and aspirations, and allow of the widest range of subjects and the widest scope of treatment."[17] Apparently, Johnson advocates a type of New Negro eclecticism, but we need to examine more closely the force holding this rainbow coalition of blackness together. Where are the elite to rally in their efforts to "lift" the masses?

At the heart of this issue is the fact that the elite and the masses are not the same; they have fundamentally different relationships toward African American and mainstream cultural practices, different emphases on material possessions, and a variety of other distinctions. Yet members of the African American elite such as Johnson subscribed to a concept that could allow the bourgeoisie to mitigate intraracial difference; it is what I shall call "race consciousness" or "race pride." "Race consciousness" is itself a splitting of black identity; moreover, it serves as an example of the performative nature of "race" as a concept by having within it an implicit acknowledgment of difference. That is, race consciousness is a process by which one moves to bridge gaps within a racial categorization by latching onto certain commonalities such as skin color or a shared history of slavery and oppression. The development of race consciousness may also involve positing and writing oneself into a discourse of community. It is a construction of race that has significant implications for race authenticity and identity. Race consciousness, particularly when employed by members of the African American elite, also expresses certain ambivalences toward class, gender, and geography, as we shall see in this and subsequent chapters. The rise of race pride or race consciousness carries with it the sticky problem of believing, at least to some extent, in the validity of racial categories themselves; rather than undermining blackness or whiteness by calling attention to and complicating the relationships between these categories' constitutive parts, an overly simplistic race consciousness may risk the reification of "race" and the closing out of possible coalitions across gender, class, geographic, color and other boundaries. Certain strategies of identification can lead to the strengthening of precisely the kinds of categories one might wish to overthrow.

James Weldon Johnson, as a "leader of the race," certainly maintained a sense of race consciousness, but that has not prevented attacks on, and marginalizations of, his voice within the discourse of black identity. Julian Mason, for example, writes that Johnson's "upbringing tended during his early life to shield him from race problems . . . to say nothing of that rural existence known only too well to the majority of his Southern black peers. Indeed, he had little *real knowledge* of that life until he taught in rural Georgia" (my emphasis).[18] What seems significant here is that Mason points directly to a certain distance from the African American folk. Johnson himself reports that "neither my father nor my mother . . . taught me anything directly about race."[19] He goes on to present his later insights into race and racism as mainly an acquired knowledge of a constructed system. Similarly, Mason insists on certain lived experiences as defining moments in the formation of identity; such a position, while assuming that some experiences are more racially immersing than others, also suggests that "race" is a learned category, that certain experiences need be acquired for one to become an authentically racial subject.

For me this raises a complex problem of the relationship between experience, ideology, and identity. If experience is the primary factor that shapes authentic identity, if, in the words of Hurston's Janie, we "got tuh *go* there tuh *know* there," then who becomes the arbiter of how much experience—and what kinds—are enough and proper?[20] To what degree does the privileging of experience draw attention away from the ideological building blocks of "race" and racism? Yet even the elevation of particular experiences to the primary determiners of racial authenticity still underlines the nonessential character of "race" itself, for one must gain experience over time rather than being born with it. I hope to point out over the course of this study that the ways in which many African American writers and thinkers interrogate "experience" serve to complicate— and perhaps even begin to dismantle—naturalized concepts of black and white difference.

Although fictional characters can have no "real" experience as such, much like Johnson himself, the narrator of *Ex-Colored Man* has to be taught that he is black.[21] When his teacher reveals to the class his narrator's (to him previously unknown) racial heritage, he becomes the objects of racist taunts: "Oh, you're a nigger, too" (401).[22] His mother, countering the demeaning epithet, assures him he's not a "nigger," but neither can she "comfort" him with the fact of being white. Her reaction is important because it emphasizes the narrator's class status above all else: "Your father is one of the greatest men in the country" (402). Here is one factor that contributes to the narrator's sense of (in)authenticity that emerges more fully later in the text. His mother emphasizes class over "race," but she refuses to give that class status an explicit racial designation of whiteness. Further, she refuses explicitly to acknowledge her own blackness, opting to emphasize the patrilineal and class-based over the matrilineal and race-based in helping her son construct his sense of self. In voicing her son's heritage in this fashion, she tacitly acknowledges whiteness as a nonracial condition. That is, she makes the narrator less of a "nigger" and more normative, although it is clear that the state—in the form of the school— and the schoolchildren do not necessarily place any stock in this kind of linguistic racial metamorphosis. At the same time, she fails to disrupt a discursive continuity between blackness and "nigger"-ness and all the implicit baggage the term carries. The narrator's mother cannot provide any vision of an authentic, realizable African American identity outside of the demeaning; moreover, she refuses to say, in fact, what her son *is* with respect to his "race," leaving the narrator's initial question unanswered in terms of its implicit query: "What race do I belong to?" Her attempt to avoid the discourse of "race," her resistance to an unambiguous categorization, winds up placing the narrator in a position of having to decide for himself what types of racial roles he wants to play.

Although the narrator claims that from that point on, "I looked out through other eyes, my thoughts were coloured, my words dictated, my actions limited by one dominating, all-pervading idea" (403), the situation is actually more complex. Certainly, being black "for the first time" — or at any time — in a racist society does limit speech and action, yet the narrator also has a sense of being different from a "regular" sort of blackness suggested in his mother's response. She instructs him in his difference from African Americans as much as the school insists on his difference from whites, and this bit of information affects his life in unique ways from that day forward. Indeed, not only does this mark a moment in which the narrator recognizes at least the possibility of multiple authentic African American subject positions, but it also functions as a recognition that whiteness too may be a racial category, one to which the narrator also has access because of the "failure" of "race" to inscribe itself on his body in the expected way. Yet initially he is more concerned with discovering what it means for him to be categorized as African American, a task further complicated by his internalized sense of difference from "real" black folks. Here within the narrator emerges a "gap in blackness" — a recognition of heterogeneity — that necessitates his later "race consciousness."

Within the context of a Euro-privileging racist society, the concept of passing also sheds light on the performative nature of "race" and its relation to a learned "authenticity." If differences of class and color separate the narrator from certain formulations of black identity, they also bring him in closer proximity to whiteness. Berzon describes passing by characters in early-twentieth-century literary works:

> Since very light-skinned blacks are often treated as white by the dominant caste, they often identify with the latter's culture and many are unwilling or unable to give up this identification and form another. They choose or have been driven to choose to continue that identification and assimilate into the dominant caste by passing for white.[23]

This passage suggests both an essential racial makeup that passers are denying by opting to live as whites and a performative nature of "race" in that racial identification may be shifted from one group to another by an individual passer. Through the state's racial categorization, the narrator is denied the possibility of assimilation, yet the arbitrary nature of black-white division is also brought into view. By unconsciously passing in his youth, the narrator begins to understand how the color line might be undermined. For passing to be a valid concept at all, it must assume racial essence; for if it did not, we could only ask, "passing for what?" Passing requires a cultural fixing of racial boundaries while also making significant links between color and culture. That is, to pass for white, one must "hide" those inherent markers of blackness (which are in fact cultural patterns of behavior) to succeed. Moreover, the logic of passing assumes that whiteness is itself "racial"; otherwise what integrity could be breached by such a performative act? Could an African American "pass" for white if she or he did not have a concept of black identity to begin with? Without that sense, what would there be to pass from and pass into?

I wonder, though, what such a notion of passing assumes about the construction of "race." Can one simply reject a racial identity and assume another merely on the basis of appearance? Or, as appears more likely to me, is passing made possible only by a solid set of criteria for racial identity? The narrator, on his return from Europe, encounters a situation that sheds some light on this problem. Discussing with an African American gentleman racism encountered aboard the ocean liner, the narrator relates, "In referring to the race I used the personal pronoun 'we'; my companion made no comment about it, nor evinced any surprise, except to raise his eyebrows slightly the first time he caught the significance of the word" (476). That small gesture, however, is enough. The passenger's surprise demonstrates that although appearance seems to be able to determine racial classification, there is more to it than that. The narrator, while not "passing" for black, must necessarily assert his blackness; a verbal performance of race is the only way for him to pass into this community of two. This incident illuminates the ways in which people—black and white— look for performed moments to know with whom they speak. Of course, the narrator's particular case of necessary performance is made more obvious by the fact that his physical signifiers of "race" do not match those expected of cultural racial discourse. Still, this kind of performance is not at all incongruous with the kinds of problems faced by phenotypically dark-skinned African Americans who have to contend with charges of being "too black" or "not black enough." Their perceived authenticity lies, like that of Johnson's narrator, in being able to negotiate specific behaviors and cultural codes that will allow others to categorize them "properly."

In 1918, Edward Byron Reuter, a white American and notorious racist, published a book in which he asserted that "the desire of the mixed-blood man is always and everywhere to be a white man; to be classified with and become a part of the superior white race."[24] Reuter goes on to suggest that all peoples of mixed racial heritage feverishly attempt to obscure and obliterate any marks of blackness, physical or cultural, they might carry with them. More than just outward appearance, passing becomes a matter of fluency in another culture's system of codes, symbols, and practices; this by no means precludes the possibility of cultural bilingualism, the ability to function successfully in both majority-black and majority-white surroundings. However, it does raise questions of authenticity: how much must one know about or publicly practice a culture's codes not to be considered a foreigner in that culture? Where do we draw the line between a convincing racial performance and a flop? The narrator of *Ex-Colored Man* takes aim at the codes informing discourses of racial identity and shows where they fail in offering a system that can distinguish with precision black from white.

When the narrator writes in the first paragraph, "I find a sort of savage and diabolical desire to gather up the tragedies of my life, and turn them into a practical joke on society" (393), he is flaunting his cultural bilingualism. By doing so, he begins to break down notions that help link blackness and whiteness to specific, distinct cultures. He plays with and on the color line in such a way that he in fact endangers the existence and validity of that line itself. To play his joke, he must create a convincing performance of racial identity that does not conform wholly to mainstream visions. The strength of his narrative voice derives from his position of (in)authenticity: he is black and he isn't; he is white and he isn't, according to the privileged discourses of racial identity.[25] His joke is to play out the consequences of such constructions of race and show how they shape our thought in odd ways. Indeed, Jean Toomer, Nella Larsen, and George Schuyler all explore the liminality of (in)authenticity, manipulating the boundaries of racial categories and identities in such ways as to call them into question.

What I find as important as *why* Johnson's narrator decides to pass is *how* he is able to do it. How is he able to learn cultural bilingualism and eventually convincingly inauthenticate himself as a black man? What factors enable him to adopt mutable racial identities? In answering these questions, I shall return to what I identified earlier as three major contributing factors to black authenticity: geography, gender, and class. I particularly want to emphasize class. In examining the ways in which these concepts are employed in *The Autobiography of an Ex-Colored Man,* I shall point out how Johnson's narrator is both inauthentic and always authentic, both colored and ex-colored.

The third paragraph of the novel begins: "I was born in a little town in Georgia a few years after the Civil War" (393). The statement places the narrator in a context that contributes to our sense of the speaker's racial authenticity. He does not come from a long line of free northern mulatto "gentry" but rather has his origins in—or near—the African American masses, in the South, with the legacy of slavery ever present in the setting. Quickly, though, the scene shifts, and as soon as the narrator can note that he "watched through the train window the corn- and cotton-fields pass swiftly" (395), we arrive in Connecticut, where the narrator states that he and his mother "lived together in a little cottage . . . fitted up almost luxuriously" (395). He describes the trappings of a bourgeois home and declares that "my mother dressed me very neatly, and I developed that pride which well-dressed boys generally have. She was careful about my associates, and I myself was quite particular. As I look back now I can see that I was a perfect little aristocrat" (395). The shift in geography also marks a shift in class status; by moving north, the narrator and his mother distance themselves from slavery, one of the main reference points for African American identity, and Johnson is able to stress the formative nature of class background on identity. With regard to *Ex-Colored Man,* though, I view this literary choice as being of great import; in quickly relocating his narrator to the North and later returning him to the South, Johnson sets up the possibility of demonstrating how different environments help create different notions of race.

Bernard Bell comments that "most of the episodes in the South reveal the narrator's acceptance of the puritan ethic of thrift, cleanliness, industry, and sobriety."[26] That is, they demonstrate the extent to which he has associated himself with notions of whiteness; puritanism implies a distance from traditional African American culture and an immersion in more mainstream middle-class Anglo-American ways of thinking. And whereas the traits Bell describes as puritan can be deemed undesirable, the suggestion is that they also serve to distance the narrator from the conditions of the African American folk. They are characteristics foisted on the narrator by virtue of his sojourn in New England geography, and they serve as an obstacle to his identification with certain notions of blackness. Although it is undeniable that the narrator exhibits a certain distaste for people who do not exhibit these traits, he also maintains a missionary and reformist attitude toward them, stating, "It is not at all a hopeless class; for these men are but creatures of condition" (435). The partial goal of any "uplift" pursued by the narrator would be to "raise" this element of the folk to a level on par with his own upbringing. At this stage, the narrator is attempting to change the discourse of black identity to suit himself as much as he is trying to write himself into a conception of black folk. It is a project, however, that never quite succeeds.

It seems as if Yankee industry, at least at this critical moment, is incompatible with the dominant discourse of black identity; Yankee class values serve only to alienate the narrator from a folk-based notion of blackness. He is not assigned inauthentic status merely by his decision to pass but is doomed from the outset by virtue of his class background. One should note as well that Johnson, Toomer, Larsen, and Schuyler all tend to focus on northern bourgeois narrators, those who lack certain experiences constitutive of folk authenticity. In choosing to portray these characters as central, the authors bring to the fore the relationship between lived experience and the politics of representation. They challenge us to rethink whether we can employ a naturalized notion of " 'how life is really like out there' as a kind of test against which the political rightness or wrongness of a particular cultural strategy or text can be measured."[27] Attacking this issue from various angles, these authors highlight the self-conscious remaking of, and struggle with, African American identity and art in the Harlem Renaissance; they busily offer new possibilities for New Negro identity.

When Johnson's narrator asserts that "log-cabins and plantations and dialect-speaking 'darkies' are perhaps better known in American literature than any other single picture of our national life" while lamenting that a "novel dealing with coloured people who live in respectable homes and amidst a fair degree of culture and who naturally acted 'just like white folks' would be taken in a comic opera sense" (486), he calls attention to the sort of class privilege inherent in the dominant discourse of black identity. To be black and bourgeois is absurd; it is "putting on airs" that are not authentically black. By virtue of his class affinities, Johnson's narrator is pushed away from black identity.

Despite being out of the mainstream in terms of the discourse of black identity, Johnson insists throughout the novel on the possibility of being both black and middle-class. Shiny, whom the narrator teases before he is educated about his own racial heritage, becomes an important symbol for blackness in the novel, developing into a touchstone for a certain type of authenticity, antithetical to purely class-based folk authenticity. The narrator's attraction to Shiny stems from the fact that " 'Shiny' was considered without question to be the best speller, the best reader, the best penman—in a word, the best scholar, in the class. . . . Yet it did not take me long to discover that, in spite of his standing as a scholar, he was in some way looked down upon" (399). For the young narrator, Shiny is attractive as a proto–Talented Tenth figure. He is educated and articulate but suffers under a second-class status on the basis of race, which in Shiny's case, is all the more evident by virtue of pigmentation. Yet after instruction in his own background, the narrator holds Shiny up as a model of African American deportment; the narrator takes him as a sort of role model, and Shiny becomes a peculiar connection to the masses. While seeing him as part of the exceptional few, the narrator also looks at Shiny's skin and uses it to connect with the folk. Describing the effects of Shiny's valedictory speech, the narrator writes:

> I felt leap within me pride that I was coloured; and I began to form wild dreams of bringing glory and honour to the Negro race. For days I could talk of nothing else with my mother except for my ambitions to be a great man, a great coloured man, to reflect credit on the race and gain fame for myself. (417)

Visible blackness, the grossest trope of white racism—and the kind of blackness that normally cannot be convincingly performed—becomes a catalyst for the narrator in embracing his own African American back-ground.[28] Shiny's intellectual and oratorical talents give the narrator a sense that blackness can be equivalent to greatness; authenticity is not necessarily tied to second-class status. In the face of Shiny's unmistakable racial connection, the narrator flirts with writing himself more defini-tively into the discourse of blackness. The intellectual becomes the racial, thereby offering a whole new range of possibilities. Via specific ideas and thoughts, one can work toward writing oneself into a discourse of black-ness despite the signifiers of "race" appearing on the body; as a corollary, Shiny writes himself out of the identity of "nigger" in part through his scholastic achievements. As a white-appearing person raised in bourgeois surroundings, however, the narrator has a difficult time of it; the lure of simply blending into the white world "unnoticed"—of refusing to per-form blackness of any sort by performing only whiteness—remains ever present.

At the same time that Shiny provides him with ambition toward a new connection with blackness, the narrator turns to two other male charac-ters in shaping his own identity. Interestingly, both of them are white: his father and his millionaire friend. The white male world is, for the narra-tor, primarily a realm of money.[29] The perception begins with a ten-dollar gold piece given to the narrator by his father on the boy's departure from the South and continues through the end of the novel, at which point the narrator is passing for a white real estate speculator. Or, more pre-cisely, he is passing for white (though, of course, the concept of passing is itself paradoxical) while he *is* a real estate speculator. This world of money stands in direct contrast to the image of blackness as lower-class. This is an important intersection of class, race, and gender; Johnson constructs a world in which wealth is synonymous with the white male. The challenge for the narrator is to rise in class status without losing African American identity. The narrator wants to become more like his millionaire mentor and remain black at the same time. Further, by performing this class-based "whiteness," the narrator can possibly begin to deconstruct the racist cul-tural codes that link race with class. He mixes and matches racial signifiers, thereby exhibiting their instability as markers of "authentic" difference. This desire to move toward the middle (or even upper) class is a major determinant of the narrator's heritage of culture and identity; the wealthy white mentor is, in Julian Mason's estimation, "a truer father than his

Southern one . . . [since his benefactor] encourages him in his music and provides for him a life of luxury and opportunities for travel and for general enrichment."[30] If the narrator's genetic heritage is mulatto, then his cultural ancestry is certainly "culturally mulatto," a mixing of factors such as class and geography that are traditionally associated with one race or another.[31] The narrator's mentor influences his attitudes toward culture and status, but that infusion of "white" values does not make for a white, or even inauthentically black, African American.

Performances of alternate African American subjectivities, like those of certain "uplift" ideologies, can be destructive of certain types of African American identity. At the same time, however, such performances may have as their goal the deconstruction of particular notions of "whiteness." John Mencke points out that an author who focuses on the African American middle class is not necessarily attempting to denigrate some notion of the folk. Mencke declares that episodes in novels that extol the virtues of the African American middle class do not have as their purpose

> merely to criticize the behavior of lower-class blacks. . . . More important, they served as devices for showing white readers that all Negroes were not alike. . . . Indeed, the ultimate purpose of all the exaggerated characterizations of mulatto figures as paragons of middle-class (white) virtues was the desire of bridging *caste* distinctions with *class* affinities.[32]

Mencke will not go so far as to validate bourgeois status as authentic black subjectivity, but he does acknowledge that class is a major marker of difference within the black community. A vision of the folk may still be the touchstone for understanding "the black condition," but the performance of certain "less authentic" African American subject positions can function as a weapon against racist ideologies that restrict African Americans in myriad ways.

Mencke sees this impulse toward middle-class representation as directed toward whites; to be sure, many portrayals of the black bourgeoisie had this goal in mind. In *Ex-Colored Man,* Johnson's narrator makes a similar point when he states:

> I think that the white people somehow feel that colored people who have education and money, who wear good clothes and live in com-

fortable houses are "putting on airs," that they do these things for the sole purpose of "spiting the white folks," or are, at best, going through a sort of monkey-like imitation. . . . It seems that the whites have not yet been able to realize and understand that these people in striving to better their physical and social surroundings in accordance with their financial and intellectual progress are simply obeying an impulse which is common to human nature the world over. (436–37)

The narrator directs his comments toward white acceptance of a black bourgeoisie (that is, people impinging on "white" territory), but I cannot help but hear a message directed at African Americans here. Racist ideology sets the parameters of performance; the script as it stands is inherently antiblack. Moreover, "race" and racism are learned behaviors that serve to preserve the status quo. Should African Americans challenge established notions of proper racial performance—say, those linking race and class—they also have the opportunity to challenge ideas about "race" itself and disrupt racist ideologies and institutions. By specifically directing his points about class distinctions to a white audience, however, the narrator seeks to preserve a race consciousness that he hopes will keep him tied closely to the African American folk and black identity.

To make this point more precise, I quote here a passage from *Ex-Colored Man* that precedes a section of the novel for which Johnson is frequently criticized: "The coloured people may be said to be roughly divided into three classes, *not so much in respect to themselves as in respect to their relations with whites*" (434, my emphasis). He goes on with the oft-quoted description of "the desperate class" (434), the second class of "all who are connected with whites in domestic service" (435), and the third class of "independent workmen and tradesmen, and of the well-to-do and educated coloured people" (436). And although the narrator does indeed attack the behaviors of lower-class African Americans, revealing perhaps an "honest but nevertheless tragically reactionary expression of class prejudice," he never questions their authenticity.[33] He presses class prejudice into the service of exploding a limiting version of the discourse of black identity. He is interested less in defining one group as more black than another than in investing his energies in expanding the boundaries of possible black identity.

While commenting on intraracial differences resulting from class standing, the narrator invokes status and blackness in ways that do not make them mutually exclusive:

> If the mass of Negroes took their present and future as seriously as do most of their leaders, the race would be in no mental condition to sustain the terrible pressure it undergoes; it would sink of its own weight. Yet it must be acknowledged that in the making of a race over-seriousness is a far lesser failing than its reverse, and even the faults resulting from it lean toward the right. (495)

The folk and the bourgeoisie may have contrasting reactions to the "making of a race" (note the interesting use of "race" as a construction), but neither holds the monopoly on black authenticity. In fact, here again the narrator works to shift the discourse of African American identity toward the bourgeoisie. Not only is middle-class status authentic, but it is necessary for political mobilization. I view this not as much as an attempt to wrest black authenticity away from the folk as an effort to create a shared authenticity that would allow easier advancement of a middle-class agenda.

Although it seems somewhat to contradict his earlier statements on his developing racial identity, the narrator's proclamation on middle-class African American society during his sojourn in Jacksonville marks explicitly the possibility of real nonfolk experience:

> Through my music teaching and my not absolutely irregular attendance at church I became acquainted with the best class of coloured people in Jacksonville. This was really my entrance into the race. It was my initiation into what I have termed the freemasonry of the race. I had formulated a theory of what it was to be colored; now I was getting practice. The novelty of my position caused me to observe and consider things which, I think, entirely escaped the young men I associated with; or, at least, were so commonplace to them as not to attract their attention. (433)

That the narrator takes as his initiation to black identity his association with the "best class of coloured people" is not necessarily an indictment of the folk-cultural practices. After all, he needs ragtime, for example, to cement his connection with black identity even more firmly. The passage, however, is yet another marker of difference within the African American community. Although they may share in racial oppression regardless of status, all blacks are not created equal in the narrator's eyes. The folk are useful in terms of understanding African American history and garnering a sense of black identity, but they remain too distant in terms of experience and custom for him to consider himself a part of that group. What is significant about this passage is not only the way in which the narrator constructs himself as a member of, and participant in, a notion of blackness, but also the way in which he constructs himself as separate from, and an observer of, the "race." Here he continues to build for himself an (in)authentic identity. Lacking the folk experience and proximity to folk culture that would allow him to participate fully in that discourse of black identity, he employs his position as an outsider to explore the politics of race and the pitfalls of connecting color identity and culture while also using that position to lay the foundation for a bourgeois-directed vision of black advancement.

This self-conscious split is perhaps one of the key aspects of *The Autobiography of an Ex-Colored Man*. The narrator becomes both authentic and inauthentic in that through his race consciousness if nothing else, he finds a connection with the trials and triumphs of African American culture while simultaneously creating a detached persona. It is through the "inauthentic" subject position that the narrator observes and comments on the state of race relations in America. He can write from this position, in some moments of the novel, as if he were not "racial" at all, as if the things he describes about race relations and African American culture have no bearing on him whatsoever. For example, when he says, "the coloured man looked at everything through the prism of his relationship to society as a *coloured* man" (434), the narrator is engaging in exactly the observational split I am attempting to explain. His use of the third person indicates a strategic stepping away from racial identification in order to explicate its consequences. He affects a nonblack, nonracial identity, indeed inauthenticates himself, so that he can look at the world through more than just the prism of race. This is a new aspect of his performance, in which the narrator attempts to write himself out of "race"—since, given his experience, he recognizes that neither whites nor blacks have the ability to see "objectively" without the shadings of their "race" coloring their view—in an effort to become an "objective" commentator on the role "race" plays in the United States. It is a strategic performance that plays on and questions discourses of both black and white identity; after all, the colored person sees things as a colored person only because she or he has been subjected to the white (and equally racial) person's system that created that difference in the first place.

Indeed, this pattern of identification and disengagement prevails throughout the book. Johnson's narrator alternately embraces and pushes away African American identity, particularly with respect to the black folk and its position within the hierarchy of authentic visions of blackness. Bell notes that the narrator "fluctuates between feelings of shame and pride in his racial identity."[34] I submit that this fluctuation is largely a result of his varying stances as producer-participant and observer-consumer of African American culture. The narrator adeptly performs these two identities and consequently discovers a paradox of racial identity as it is configured from his class, gender, and geographic background. I shall return to this paradox later on, but now I want to observe some specific instances in which the narrator invokes his producer-participant and consumer-observer identities.

Because he is a musician and composer, one of the narrator's deepest interests in African American culture comes, naturally, in the area of music. And it is on the basis of his relationship with traditional forms of African American music that one may observe the ways in which he participates in an "authentic" folk culture. The narrator gains fame in New York by playing ragtime piano; he describes ragtime as a style that "originated in the questionable resorts about Memphis and St. Louis by Negro piano-players who knew no more of the theory of music than they did of the theory of the universe, but were guided by natural musical instinct and talent" (447).[35] By learning to play ragtime, he writes himself, literally performs himself, into a "natural" type of racial identity from which he can also conveniently keep his distance. One might say—returning to the producer-participant-observer-consumer complexity of the narrator's character—that what the reader finds here is an instance of the appropriation of African American folk culture.

Eric Lott, in his book *Love and Theft: Blackface Minstrelsy and the American Working Class,* has made some excellent historical and theoretical points about the commodification of African American folk culture across the color line. What strikes me in Johnson's case, however, are the possible implications of appropriation *within* racial borders but *across* an intraracial class divide.[36] Lott writes that "the cultural forms of the black dispossessed in the United States have been appropriated and circulated as stand-ins for a supposedly national folk tradition. . . . The first appearance in U.S. history of black culture as property was blackface minstrelsy's marketing of an internally differentiated cultural 'blackness.'"[37] Yet unless we deny Johnson's narrator an African American subject position, we find here an even more complex situation. Ragtime becomes not simply an appropriable stand-in for American folk tradition or an authentic marker of black-white difference but a highly constructed notion of class-inflected racial identity itself. It is, perhaps, only by engaging in a kind of minstrel appropriation of his own culture that the narrator can garner a sense of "natural" identity. The very act of having to learn ragtime points out the place of difference within any sense of cultural blackness, and the possibility (and for the narrator even the necessity) of multiple simultaneous authentic African American subject positions. Through the performance of a black bourgeois musician, Johnson begins to blur the boundaries of black and white that remain too often unquestioned in much of our thinking.

By performing folk identity, one also has the opportunity of leaving it. Of course, the narrator is particularly proud of his transcriptions of Western classics by Beethoven, Mendelssohn, and Chopin into the ragtime style. The narrator cannot divorce himself from certain European traditions, but he becomes a producer of a particularly African American style by "blackening" these classics. He adopts them to his own unique, "racial" style rather than seeing them as sacred and untouchable. Indeed, we find here yet another form of appropriation that suggests the viability of a discourse of black identity somewhere between the "inauthenticity" of European high culture and the "authenticity" of African American vernacular culture.

Another important aspect of his interest in African American music is, as Huggins points out, the narrator's belief that "musical talent is really ethnic."[38] Although this belief is, indeed, quite a pernicious racial stereotype, it is through this stereotype that the narrator seeks to prove his authentic blackness. Because he can play the piano not only in classical but in the black vernacular fashion, he can construct himself as an authentically racial being. Ragtime lends him a proximity to folk tradition that helps develop a particular black identity, and although he continually has an impulse toward "high," or Western, culture, the narrator's participation in folk cultural forms aids in providing an entrée into the discourse of blackness. Given the narrators's position outside the African American folk, must we not see him as engaging, at least at some level, in precisely the kind of appropriation as the white minstrel performer? Doesn't the black middle class *necessarily* put on a type of minstrel mask every time it writes itself into or performs folk identity? Yet unlike the white minstrel performer who comes to the club to glean songs and behaviors for performances designed to amuse in their comic approximations of blackness and with the consequence of "stall[ing] the development of African-American public arts and generat[ing] an enduring narrative of racist ideology," Johnson's narrator is the "real thing" attempting to gain an identity and make an antiracist cultural statement by learning how to perform in a properly "racial" manner.[39] The narrator is seeking to promote African American "genius" and culture rather than ridicule it. The irony, of course, is that such a performance really serves to highlight just how highly constructed and performed any notion of racial or cultural identity is. In the metaphor of the minstrel show (as we shall see in Larsen and Schuyler) or the theater (as we shall see in Toomer), we can begin to see how discourses of authentic black identity are codified in specifically performative ways.[40]

On his return from Europe, the narrator undertakes a study of southern music in the African American tradition. He explains his interest in the following manner:

> As yet, the Negroes themselves do not fully appreciate these old slave songs. The educated classes are rather ashamed of them and prefer to sing hymns from books. This feeling is natural; they are still too close to the conditions under which the songs were produced; but the day will come when this slave music will be the most treasured heritage of the American Negro. (494)

Here we see another example of the narrator disassociating himself, through the use of the third person, from particular aspects of black identity. It is significant at this moment, however, that he speaks from a position of pride and, indeed, empathy—perhaps even an identification— with the southern rural folk. The narrator takes as his mission to bring folk forms of culture to every class of African American and in doing so finds a way to force himself into the discourse of black (folk) identity.

In this way, Johnson's narrator not only echoes the northern bourgeois DuBois in *The Souls of Black Folk* but also prefigures middle-class Harlem Renaissance figures such as Alain Locke in his elevation and valorization of folk cultural forms. Dickson Bruce has suggested that for poetry written in this era, such a move is not unusual for an African American writer; rehabilitation of the South as a central image of black life was done "with a full knowledge of both the good and evil of Southern life . . . [and] these poets stressed their own realism and sought to impute it to a class of people, the 'folk Negroes' of the South."[41] Whereas Johnson's narrator can chastise white southern racism and black southern "backwardness," he also views southern black folk culture as a source of strength and pride for every group of African Americans. By participating in that tradition, the narrator, in his own mind, not only lends value to folk culture but also adds value to his own identity. This identification with the folk is, in many respects, the "birthright" Johnson's narrator laments at the end of the novel. And although Huggins believes that *Ex-Colored Man* ends regrettably with "the Negro soul denied," I submit that such denial is not necessarily a tragic end, but rather part of an ongoing process for a character seeking a voice in the discourse of blackness that privileges a class status of which the narrator is not part.[42] Ironically, even in the moments of uplift and race consciousness during which he argues for a more middle-class conception of black identity, the narrator reproduces the very primacy of the folk—by making it the central object of his struggle—he is attempting to reduce. Again this emphasis on folk culture is a component of the narrator's race consciousness, his bridging of class and geographic distances among African Americans through the study of specifically African American cultural forms. And Eugene Levy has pointed out:

> Johnson believed that the acceptance by the American public of black music and black musicians not only demonstrated the ability of the race but also encouraged race pride. Yet despite this belief, Johnson had little direct contact with the black culture of which that music was an expression, and he remained firmly committed to accepted American values, musical and otherwise.[43]

Extrapolating from Levy's comment on Johnson suggests that the narrator's authenticity in terms of a southern rural folk is dubious at best. At the same time, however, it is through this distance that the narrator

positions himself as a "race leader." As an observer-consumer of folk culture—one who sees it as an exploitable resource more than an inherent or
"natural" part of the self—rather than a full participant in it, the narrator
risks classification as inauthentically black, yet it is through this consumption of cultural forms that he creates a sense of African American identity.
Here Johnson's paradox of race emerges again; participation in the most
"authentic" cultural forms may be central to the formation of identity,
but factors of class also alienate him from that authenticity. Racial identity is at odds with circumstances of origin and upbringing; the narrator
becomes (in)authentic, both a part of, and distant from, that most "real"
of all African American identities, the folk.

As a result of (in)authenticity, the narrator uses his position of class,
geography, and gender to become a guardian of folk culture. From his
position as an outsider, folk culture becomes a resource to be preserved
and doled out at strategic political moments. Indeed, Julian Mason explains that along with Charles Chesnutt, Johnson "can be given credit for
preserving Southern folk materials"[44] although he rejects that identity for
one "more urban and high culture, more elite and cosmopolitan in orientation."[45] When in *Ex-Colored Man* the narrator states that "the coloured
people of this country have done four things . . . which demonstrate they
have originality and artistic conception, and, what is more, the power of
creating that which can influence and appeal universally" (440), he cites
examples of folk culture: folktales, the Jubilee songs made popular by the
Fisk singers, ragtime, and the cakewalk. None of these forms are specific
to the narrator's Connecticut upbringing, but he embraces them as central
to his own identity and black identity in general. Stephen Bronz has suggested that Johnson's similar position toward folk culture demonstrated
his ability "to love and enjoy the life of the people he was trying to uplift."[46] Whereas this may indeed be true for both Johnson and his narrator
in *Ex-Colored Man,* this use of the folk also underlines differences among
African Americans. And it is this insistence on difference that best charac-
terizes the tone of the novel.

The narrator's wealthy benefactor reinforces the narrator's positionality
as (in)authentically black. In an oft-quoted passage, the millionaire declares,

My boy, you are by blood, by appearance, by education, and by
tastes a white man. Now why do you want to throw your life away

amidst the poverty and ignorance, in the hopeless struggle, of the black people in the United States? . . . This idea of you making a Negro of yourself is nothing more than a sentiment; and you do not realize the fearful import of what you intend to do. What kind of Negro would you make now, especially in the South? (472–73)

The narrator stands outside the "mainstream" of blackness, yet he insists on maintaining — at least at this point — an African American identity. Despite the benefactor's comments, the narrator moves to acknowledge and strengthen his blackness. He resists the restrictive classification. Class and geographic position and gender privilege allow the narrator to distance himself from the majority of black Americans, yet that distance in itself does not necessarily disqualify him as an African American. Race identity simply cannot be erased because one is a minority within a minority. The narrator's various racial identifications are primarily matters of choice, of invoking class, geography, and gender in certain manners for specific purposes. It is in this way that *The Autobiography of an Ex-Colored Man* has its most important resonances for notions of race and racial authenticity in African American literature.

The narrator can either participate in, or divorce himself from, cultural practices that lead others to classify him in terms of "race." What, then, does that say about the nature of "race" as configured in *The Autobiography of an Ex-Colored Man?* What makes one colored, uncolored, or ex-colored? I suggest that the relative ease with which the narrator can accept or reject black identity emphasizes the learned nature of race; nurture, it seems, contributes more to racial authenticity than does some inherent, innate, or instinctual biological nature. Although the narrator may imply that his musical talents are a natural gift of his race, he still has to seek out specific musical forms that allow him to identify with blackness. It is folk music that lends racial authenticity, not mere musical talent.

Johnson primarily considers "race" in the abstract, as an equation derived from a set of variables that include class, gender, and geography. "Race" becomes more a notion to be studied and manipulated more than a deterministic essence. Although "race" can determine consciousness in a DuBoisian sense, not every African American's consciousness will be identical even though some are considered more authentic than others.

Even in the lynching scene toward the end of *Ex-Colored Man,* the narrator takes a curious stand with regard to his racial identity. Recognizing that mere skin color is motive enough for murder, he first experiences "shame that [he] belonged to a race that could be so dealt with" (497). He has learned the dynamics of racism well enough to see the extent to which Eurocentric notions of "race" define him, in spite of his refinement. The act of lynching places him squarely in the black community, defining him from without; white racism shows it cares not a whit for his sophisticated notions of performance. His next action, however, is to disassociate himself from blackness; he performs his (in)authenticity, moving African Americans to the third person in his discourse: "I can understand why Negroes sympathize. . . . *they* can and should do nothing less" (497–98, my emphasis). The narrator again plays gross notions of "racial" identity to his advantage, pitting his learned racial identity and his phenotypical indeterminacy against the essentialist finality of the lynch mob; it is a scene that George Schuyler will amplify with satiric glee in *Black No More* when he portrays the lynching of white men in blackface. The narrator's "different" type of blackness becomes his means of escape from the terror of racism, the irony of this all being that in passing, he risks his own economic, if not physical, lynching should he be discovered. He challenges deadly conceptions of difference by defying racialists to spot his. Confident in his ability to perform codes of "racial" behavior, however, the narrator is fairly sure that his "true" identity—in terms of blackness in a racist society—will never be discovered. His (in)authenticity provides temporary refuge.

It is precisely at this point of determining this authenticity of consciousness that Johnson's narrator seems most undecided. The narrator can go through the book championing both the greatness of certain folk-cultural forms and the special role of the black bourgeoisie, but his final lament that he "sold [his] birthright for a mess of pottage" (511) when he passes for white asks his readers to reexamine his stance(s) on the nature of "race." What *is* his birthright? What is that essence of blackness he implies he has given up when he passes? Huggins believes that Johnson saw this birthright not only as the "abdication of [the protagonist's] art (and his essential self) but, more, as that the society had lost the cultural synthesis that might have been possible through the genius of this marginal man."[47] Although I disagree with Huggins as to the "essential self" of the narrator (it seems to me he has spent nearly the entire novel attempting to prove the nonexistence of an essential self, at least in terms of "race") I do think that the most important loss incurred in passing is the process of thought, or "synthesis," in which the narrator is engaged. As a doubly marginal, perhaps doubly invisible, figure, the narrator loses, within the context of his fictional life, his ability to deconstruct notions of "race" when he relinquishes control of his identity.[48] Rather than trading, as Berzon suggests, his birthright of "spontaneity, creativity, and personal and racial pride for an uneasy—and often unfulfilling—identification for white middle-class America,"[49] he loses the ability to perform various identities at various moments in an effort to understand the dynamics of racial identity in the United States. The irony, of course, is that in creating this text, the narrator continues to explore exactly that issue. In writing his memoir, the narrator reclaims, at least in part, his birthright of examining, from his unique position, the building blocks and possibilities of authentic racial identity.

The act of passing does not void the narrator of blackness. Rather, it suggests that assumptions of class, gender, and geography inform our notions of race. If we are unwilling to assume widely varying types of racial authenticity, we open ourselves up to being duped. Huggins claims that Johnson's narrator "merely chooses to no longer act Negro."[50] But what the narrator really does is choose no longer to openly embrace folk forms of African American culture. His blackness—the facts of his experience and race consciousness—remains, even under the guise of whiteness. The narrator simply moves beyond commonly held notions of racial authenticity and in doing so moves into the realm of mistaken (on the part of persons who try to classify him) and protean (in terms of his self-imposed classifications) identity.

The narrator of *Ex-Colored Man* is caught in a great paradox of race; he is both part of and apart from "race." Levy declares that the narrator, in deciding to pass, "flees both the South and his race. Yet it is 'his' race and he knows it."[51] Indeed, even the title bears this idea out. "Ex-colored" is by no means an escape from black identity. The narrator cannot redefine himself in terms of whiteness ("Autobiography of a Newly White Man"), but only in terms of a negation of blackness. Blackness or coloredness remains the defining principle in his identity. Race is key to any notion of identity he might have, yet he does not mesh with common concepts of black identity, and his passing makes him a fraud as a white. Through race consciousness, the narrator draws himself closer to an "authentic" African American subject position, and only in performing aspects of that authentic identity does he keep from losing his race and, thereby, his identity. At the same time, though, he views himself as separate from both black and white authenticities, and it is through this separation, this alternate authenticity, that the narrator goes about his self-appointed task of explaining the role of "race" in the United States. The race consciousness that underlies his black identity and gives him a link to authenticity is largely a product of his inauthenticity; the narrator states that "sometimes it seems to me that I have never really been a Negro, that I have been only a privileged spectator of their inner life" (510). Without a notion of black authenticity that takes into account his class, geography, and gender, Johnson's narrator can derive a sense of authenticity only from his position as an outsider. Johnson's writing in 1912 prefigures what Stuart Hall says eighty years later:

> as always happens when we naturalize historical categories . . . we fix the signifier outside of history, outside of change, outside of political intervention. And once it is fixed, we are tempted to use "black" as sufficient in itself to guarantee the progressive character of the politics we fight under the banner. . . . We are tempted to display that signifier as a device which can purify the impure, bring straying brothers and sisters who don't know what they ought to be doing into line, and police the boundaries—which are of course political, symbolic and positional boundaries—as if they were genetic.[52]

Indeed, the narrator's lament for his birthright reflects a belief in—or a desire for—a genetic boundary that would greatly simplify his aesthetic and political actions, that would make them (and him) easily categorizable. Yet, of course, Johnson sees more than the narrator; while the latter yearns to write himself unproblematically *into "race,"* the former is more concerned with *writing "race"* and thereby further complicating the category. Johnson strives to point out how the signifier "black"—along with its inseparable companion, the signifier "white"—is always already impure because they are socially constructed and contingent on numerous other factors. For the New Negro simply to fix his or her identity on a fresh set of unchanging essentials is simply to recreate the problem of "Old Negro" identity. Even if his protagonist cannot see it, Johnson seems to understand the necessity of denaturalizing historical categories. Through the narrator's performance and change, the author moves to destabilize our knowledge of what constitutes difference.

It is inauthenticity of race that lends the narrator authentic identity; that is, an identity that forms from an amalgam of positions—color, class, gender, sexuality, geography—that refuse to be neatly aligned, that are always in negotiation and contestation. The "ex-colored" in the novel's title applies not so much to the narrator's decision to pass for white but to the fact that an older category of blackness has lost its power accurately or adequately to describe the complexity of at least one African American subject position.

# 3

"Colored; cold.

Wrong somewhere.":

Jean Toomer's *Cane*

*Without the touch of the black soul, Jean Toomer was not an artist but a scribbler.* —ROBERT H. BRINKMEYER JR., "Wasted Talent, Wasted Art"

*Toomer was an artist and artists are capable of achievements which ordinary people are not, and . . . we can't include a writer in the Afro-American literary tradition simply because of a feeling we have about his work.* —RUDOLPH P. BYRD, "Jean Toomer and the Afro-American Literary Tradition"

*Cane was for Toomer a double "swan song." He meant it to memorialize a culture he thought was dying, whose folk-spirit he considered beautiful, but he was also saying good-bye to the "Negro" he felt dying in himself. Cane then is a parting gift, and no less precious because of that. I think Jean Toomer would want us to keep its beauty, but let him go.* —ALICE WALKER, *In Search of Our Mothers' Gardens*

*A folk culture containing its own resonant harmonies, communal values and assumptions, and fruitful proximity to ancestral soil offers a starting point for the journey toward black art. The artist, however, cannot simply observe the surface beauties of this culture; he must comprehend the self-knowledge and nobility of spirit that made its creation possible in the midst of an inhuman servitude.* —HOUSTON A. BAKER JR., *Afro-American Poetics*

These various commentaries on *Cane* (1923) offer an intriguing point of departure for a discussion about the text, its author, and their relationships to concepts of "race." One of the major questions raised in considering this matrix of critics is, for me, not which one of these is "true" in its own right, but whether (and, indeed, how) they can all apply to some degree to the same relatively short text. Certainly it can be useful to seek some combination of racial characteristics that serve as *Cane*'s guiding principles, although perhaps the novel is just as much a work by an author with radical, new ideas about the construct of "race" who just happened, in this instance, to take African Americans as his subject. Whatever the case, *Cane* stands at the center of a controversy surrounding the discourse(s) of black identity. To return to the work of Stuart Hall for a moment, perhaps we can best understand the proliferation of critical opinion about *Cane* by looking at the politics of (African American) representation and their dependence on notions of black authenticity. Hall suggests that

> it is only through the way in which we represent and imagine ourselves that we come to know how we are constituted and who we are. There is no escape from the politics of representation, and we cannot wield 'how life really is out there' as a kind of test against which the political rightness or wrongness of a particular cultural strategy or text can be measured.[1]

The attempt to recuperate *Cane* and Toomer into the canon of African American literature causes a moment of crisis, for *Cane* is a text that attempts to resist such a recovery, at least one effected through unproblematized, racialist assumptions. Rather than reading *Cane* as a text whose "political rightness or wrongness" needs to be measured, I would suggest that we might profit by using the text to measure the politics and limits of our critical perspectives.

It is my position that *Cane* is a text that elicits a wide variety of critical reaction because it opens a large space in which various discourses of black identity coincide and intersect, sometimes competitively and at other times harmoniously. Jean Toomer's personal racial ambivalence, as well as the ambivalence found in the text, and these sometimes contradictory critical positions arise as a result of Toomer's embrace of the performative as a way of understanding African American identity. As he breaks with repeated and familiar patterns that delineate literary blackness, he re-imagines the shape of both the African American and American communities, exploring ways in which the traditions that define and differentiate might be reworked. As he does this, Toomer asks us to consider what criteria go into making something American or African American. How and when is something recognizably national or racial? What contributes to that intuitive "touch of soul" or "feeling" that informs artistic blackness? Louis Armstrong once quipped that you won't ever know jazz if you have to ask what it is, but to make the same case with African American literature is perhaps less productive.[2] Such a move answers few questions about discourses of black identity; rather, it simply mystifies it. Yet although Toomer does not seek to further mystify the discourse of literary blackness, I do not believe he seeks to clarify or simplify it, either. *Cane* challenges the notion that "good black . . . culture can pass the test of authenticity—the reference to black experience and to black expressivity . . . [which] serve as the guarantees in the determination of which black . . . culture is right on, which is ours and which is not."[3] Still, the critical discourse about the texts seeks to regulate it, to render it knowable, in terms of familiar—and perhaps unsatisfactory—categories.

The formulations of Brinkmeyer, Byrd, Walker, and Baker point to the need for a deeper understanding of varying discourses of black identity. I submit that these critics' divergent viewpoints stem from Toomer's own multifaceted attacks on, and embrace of, particular notions of black identity; in reimagining communities and seeking to reinvent (African) American literary tradition, Toomer "became less concerned with representing race and thereby 'liberating' it . . . than with inventing an entirely new discourse."[4]

As early as 1920, Toomer was toying with this new "race" that comprised "a blend of all European, African, Asian, and American Indian cultures."[5] In positing "American" as a new "race," one that is necessarily heterogeneous with no chance of even an imagined "purity" of essence or genetics, Toomer takes a radical step not only toward defining his place in American letters but also toward challenging racist and racialist conceptions of identity he views as hindering cultural progress. In his own lifetime, Toomer was repeatedly criticized and misunderstood with respect to this departure from traditional racial discourses. He relates one anecdote in which, after having read some work (a draft of the poem "The First American," which eventually evolved into "The Blue Meridian") to "a friend at the time, a colored fellow of more than ordinary grasp" whom Toomer thinks might understand his new racial proposition, the friend simply replies, "You're white."[6] Because Toomer refuses to act out socially "normative" racial roles, because he denies the validity of established categories, his African American friend denies Toomer authentic black racial identity. Of course, for Toomer, this is no big loss; to a "reformulator," a denial of black authenticity is hardly a slap in the face, yet the reclassification as "white" is troublesome. For him, it simply reconstructs a culturally conditioned system of "race" that leads to social strife and limiting artistic borders in the first place. Toomer himself remarks, "My dear enemies, those who like to misrepresent me, would have . . . said at once, 'Toomer wants to deny his race.'"[7] The point is, however, that there is really no race to deny in the sense that his detractors mean. His attempt to reinvent the term stands at the base of such "misrepresentation." In Toomer's eyes, racial representation of any kind often borders on misrepresentation. "Race," in the sense that he struggles against, is an inadequate term concept for the thorough contextualizing of the individual. It regulates and disciplines rather than liberates.

In 1922, Toomer wrote Claude McKay that "from my own point of view I am naturally and inevitably an American. I have strived for a spiritual fusion analogous to the fact of racial intermingling."[8] While certainly not subscribing to the one-drop theory of racial categorization, Toomer is not "denying his race" in the sense of attempting to "pass." Rather, he breaks with more familiar demarcations of difference to invent a community in which the common bond is difference itself; he imagines an America (and an American) that assumes heterogeneity as its normative condition.

In 1921, Toomer was writing a poem entitled "The First American," which later became "The Blue Meridian," published in 1936. In it he laid a groundwork for this reimagination of community, his vision of superseding "race" as he knew it through a new spirituality, miscegenation, a reinvention of the past, a reformulation of art, and the emergence of the "universal" human being. I quote from "The Blue Meridian": "We are waiting for a new people, / For the joining of men to men / And man to God."[9] Indeed, his reconceptions of community are generative, not building on contemporary notions but beginning from scratch. In fact, these old concepts of racial difference are obliterated through "blend[ing] our bodies to one flesh" (218), and while such an insistence on genetic mix-ing ironically serves to create a similarity throughout a population, it also "internalizes"—at least biologically—within each person a great deal of difference. In many ways, Toomer's call to acknowledge the relative lack of racial "purity" among Americans will be picked up again by George Schuyler; although Toomer tends to deal with the subject romantically and Schuyler satirically, both writers seize on this myth of the "unadulter-ated" racial being in an effort to dismantle naturalized discourses of racial identity.

Further, any maintenance of externalized, essentialized difference could only prove negative to the new America; it is a reminder of the social order based on hierarchies of difference and animosities toward fellow humans that Toomer describes as "hell / Rushing us, sweeping us, / Winding us, blinding us, / Mistakes and hates, / Habits, blights, and greeds, / out of our past they come / And they are hell" (219). In the "old" America, the one contemporary with Toomer, difference is divisive, and animosity be-tween people is perhaps fundamental; within the new America, however, the artist espouses difference ("Upon my phonograph are many records / Played on sides in sacred and profane extremes"), embracing cultural forms as different as Gregorian chants, Bach, Duke Ellington, and Eddy Duchin in an effort to create a new art for "people identical in being" (228). That is, a group of people "linked with all who ever lived" (232) in a transracial, transgeographical bond. And it is this sort of imagined com-munity that lurks somewhere beneath the surface of *Cane*.

Does Toomer's alternate formulation of "race" and identity mean, however, that he has no sense of blackness or African American culture? I suggest that his "raceless" position necessarily grows out of a consider-ation of the racist and racialist society that surrounded him throughout his youth. The "American race" did not spring into existence *ab nihilo* but rather had its roots in Toomer's experiences among, and reactions to, vari-ous "racial" cultures of his time. A product of both black and white bour-geois neighborhoods, Toomer rejected a color-based racial essence in favor of a class-based, transracial similarity. He writes of the black middle class:

> With one or two exceptions, those of my new friends who became my best friends were, in a racial sense, no different from the boys and girls I had known in white groups. They behaved as American

youths of that age and class. Their quality of person was considerably higher than the majority of boys and girls I had played with in the New York region. For this reason I felt, if anything, more at home with them. They were my kind.[10]

Class identity subsumes race identity in Toomer's experience, making the positing of racial essence all the more difficult. At the same time, however, Toomer recognizes that intraracial difference based on class, gender, and geography has been glossed over in "those whose heads ring with the rattle of race talk." The result is the continual strengthening of the black-white racial dichotomy that Toomer is attempting to resist; Toomer depends on notions of intraracial difference to lend authority to his assertion that more traditional racial distinctions are outmoded instruments of spiritual, if not social, divisiveness. He makes an interesting historical observation about the preceding passage on class affinity and the arbitrary nature of "racial" human bonds, remarking that

> this was in 1910; the movement to make the Negro self-conscious and give him racial solidarity had not yet gotten under way effectively; . . . [Moreover] no people label themselves and fix their consciousness on this label unless the thing has become ingrained in them by hearsay and education or unless external circumstances compel them to do so.[11]

Not only is Toomer positing "race" as a learned, conditioned set of attitudes and behaviors that can be enforced even by the state (a part of the compulsion he speaks of that in some ways recalls the moment of "racial discovery" Johnson's ex-colored man has in the classroom), but the formulation of "race" as race consciousness or race pride to combat external oppression can have the effect of simply reproducing a false, essentialized difference between oppressor and oppressed.[12] It would appear that at least in Toomer's view, it is precisely this elision of internal difference, this limitation placed on the discourse of identity along with a constructed insistence on fundamental interracial difference, that restricts us to seeing black or white or yellow or brown as distinct, essential entities. What becomes important in reading *Cane*, then, are the ways in which Toomer explores internal difference within the African American community. In what ways is expanding the discourse of black identity beneficial to, even the precursor of, an emerging sense of "American" identity? Only through understanding the intricacies of "race" as a functioning concept in his time can Toomer begin to dismantle it; a distinctive process leads to this broad context of the "American race," rather than creation by decree.

*Cane*'s ambiguous relationships toward "blackness" and "race" in general make the book a fruitful text for the study of the literary composition of "race." In what ways does Toomer create a literary space in which he sets in motion several often competing and contestatory discourses of black identity? Further, by highlighting the performative aspects of these discourses, how does he proceed toward a deconstruction of any one or, indeed, all of them? What can the complex figurations of racial identity in *Cane* tell us about the ways in which black identity was constructed during the Harlem Renaissance and how we have adopted and revamped that model subsequently?

In the rest of this chapter, I shall focus primarily on Toomer's geographies of blackness. Geography seems, for several reasons, the most apt place to begin discussing Toomer's influence on the discourse of black identity. First, *Cane* presents geographical movement as a key element of its overall structure. Second, several scholars have made, on the basis of reading *Cane,* a link between geography and racial identity. And third, geography is a key issue in the cultural history of African Americans, particularly in the post–World War I era during which *Cane* was written and published. Of course this list is not exhaustive, but it does, I think, offer a position from which to launch an examination of the significance of geography as a central factor in the discourse of black identity.

Charles T. Davis's essay "Jean Toomer and the South: Region and Race as Elements within a Literary Imagination" will serve as my starting point. This much-anthologized article, first published in 1974, draws attention to the centrality of geographic position to racial identity, and it does so in a way that foregrounds the African American folk. Divided into three parts (the first comprising poems and vignettes set in rural Georgia, the second dealing primarily with characters located in Washington, D.C., and other settings in the urban North, and the third part, "Kabnis," the story of a northerner in rural Georgia), *Cane* offers within its very structure specific geographic distinctions. Davis writes that one of the narrative voices in the first section represents "a sophisticated intelligence yearning for completion and adequate expression and finding the means for achieving these ends in contact with the South and with a newly discovered black culture."[13] Whatever the complexity of Toomer's narrative voice, Davis suggests that voice cannot be whole without going south and embracing the type of black culture found there. Southern geographic location is a requisite component of a completed identity. Davis states that Toomer "sees the necessity for regional connection, for the Northern black to acquire the emotional strengths that black Southerners still possess, though they may be rapidly losing them."[14]

In Davis's view, the discourse of black identity not only privileges southern status but also relies on it necessarily; without the South, blackness can only be alienated. Racial identity mandates a specific geographical position, and although Cary Wintz may assert that "by the 1920's few black intellectuals still believed that the future of their race lay in the South," the discourse of black identity still insisted on the primacy of southern rural consciousness.[15] Indeed, Cynthia Kerman and Richard Eldridge have suggested that although "seldom a joiner, Toomer discovered a group sense that was bound as much by geography as by race, for he identified the black experience principally as it was manifested in the rural South."[16] Although an exclusive correlation between blackness and the South may be too presumptuous—after all, how would we explain the second and third sections of the book if that were true?—a connection between identity, performed or essential, and geography is unmistakable in *Cane*.

Given this emphasis on the South's centrality to black identity, then, one may productively read *Cane* as a partial explication of the way in which Toomer disalienated himself from the urban North and reconnected with African American community and cultural history. *Cane* functions, in some sense, as an "odyssey . . . to know the spiritual truth of life, to reconcile the beauty and the pain of . . . Afro-American heritage, and to express . . . new consciousness in the magic of the word."[17]

Toomer fosters such a view in the aforementioned letter to Claude McKay:

> Within the last two or three years, however, my growing need for artistic expression has pulled me deeper and deeper into the Negro group. . . . A visit to Georgia last fall was the starting point of almost everything of worth I have done. I heard folk-songs that came from

the lips of Negro peasants. . . . And a deep part of my nature, a part I had repressed, sprang suddenly to life and responded to them. Now I cannot conceive of myself as aloof and separated. My point of view has not changed; it has deepened, it has widened.[18]

Although it appears that Toomer eschews identity as performance at this moment, particularly in speaking of his "nature," I would like to suggest that this "reawakening" to blackness is indeed performative, whether Toomer calls it that or not. Alice Walker says of *Cane,* "Toomer *used* his 'connection' to black people only once, when it was to his advantage to do so."[19] Her formulation is important because it suggests the consciousness of Toomer's foray into Georgia. Far from being an utterly organic, inevitable occurrence, Toomer's connection to "black" geography was noticeably planned. His adoption of a folk geography is as much a type of consumption as a reconnection; Toomer goes south to gain access to part of the matrix of discourses he is creating both in *Cane* and in his developing theory of "American." In consciously seeking out a southern geography, he is engaged in the performative act of "widening" and "deepening" his own notion of identity. Concurrently, he is also acting out a reverse migration that mirrors the historical Great Migration of the period. What I find particularly interesting about Toomer's gesture is that it is repeated—that is, the northern African American subject traveling to the South—in the novels of Johnson, Larsen, and Schuyler as well. This seems to point out the necessity of rethinking geographical privilege in the reconstruction of African American authenticity.[20]

Numerous critics have read Toomer's poem "Song of the Son," which stands about midway through the first section of *Cane,* within a more organic context of a geographic renewal (perhaps even genesis) of African American consciousness. The poem becomes an emblem of the alienated black intellectual who "returns to pay homage to his heritage: the swiftly passing culture of the slave past."[21] Certainly, there is evidence within "Song of the Son" to intimate this sort of veneration of folk culture. The oft-quoted lines "Thy son, in time I have returned to thee, / Thy son I have in time returned to thee" do, indeed, imply a narrator desirous of reclaiming an element of his heritage, a prodigal son returning home.[22] At the same time, however, I would suggest that the narrator's relationship to the land to which he returns is rather more ambiguous. The poem laments on the one hand the passing of an age, perhaps even a (folk) culture ("The sun is setting on / A song-lit race of slaves" and its "plaintive soul, leaving, soon gone"), and the narrator positions himself as that age's final chronicler.

Yet it is not necessarily the narrator's acceptance or inclusion of folk heritage that allows him to stake such a position within African American culture. Rather, it is his difference from the folk that enables this rescue mission. Perhaps the best indicator of the narrator's enabling difference is in the rudimentary but unmistakable pun of "son/sun"; in a poem that begins with the imagery of "stardust glow of night," darkness ("pine-smoke air to-nite"), and racial blackness, it is more than significant that the northern, "alienated" (and light-skinned, implying mixed heritage more outwardly representative of the "American" race) son (sun) returns to the area bringing light along with him. The northern African American becomes the preserver of the southern African American. When Toomer writes, "Now just before an epoch's sun declines / Thy son, in time, I have returned to thee," the position of the narrator as enlightener and preserver is unmistakable. Indeed, there is a further religious pun in the sense of the narrator as the Savior, the New Testament's Son of Man.

Now it is only through the consciousness of the narrator, who is markedly different from the folk he addresses, that folk culture will be carried on. The folk become a plum—"one seed becomes / An everlasting song, a singing tree"—to be nourished and nurtured by the son/sun. Northern enlightenment rescues southern identity as much as, if not more than, southern geographical position provides a northern narrator with some sort of solid black identity. A "long-lost" consciousness writes itself into the discourse of blackness by absorbing southern culture; by understanding the significance of geographic difference, the narrating voice of the poem maintains a sense of blackness, placing itself in a familiar discourse of "race" while pointing out the limiting, even self-destructive (in the sense that a homogeneous Southern blackness borders on extinction), tendencies of such a concept of "race."

"Song of the Son" is a poem about the powers that reside in intraracial difference as much as a valorization of the Southern rural folk as the source of normative black identity; the South is not discounted as a marker of African American identity, but it is not the only, or even the most powerful, voice in the discourse of blackness. Although the speaker's northern consciousness is filtered through a southern geography, the poem marks a fundamental shift in the place of geography in the discourse of black identity. The South becomes a locus of history and the past rather than an indicator of the present; in this sense, the South gets remade as performable and invocable at will rather than being a primary, immediate, and always-lived marker of identity. The South becomes more a symbol of cultural tradition—a sense of the way things used to be—in such a manner that makes it, in some ways, a less dynamic and promising site for the "evolution" of blackness. Indeed, given the son's return, he appears to come back as blackness of a higher order, dependent on his "roots" but also surpassing them in some respects.

In reconfiguring these notions of geography, Toomer establishes a unique symbiosis between geographies. Not only does this move offer a rethinking of geographic hierarchies within discourses of black identity (that is, a reevaluation of the relative "authenticities" of North and South), but it establishes a link between them with a good deal of significance for a more expansive discourse of literary blackness. Northern identity is grounded in the soil of the South; southern identity cannot survive without the North. What is of even greater import, however, is the way in which Toomer moves toward creating a wider and unifying discourse by placing these potentially contestatory discourses of geography together in a matrix and demonstrating the ways in which they inform each other. All this is not to say, however, that Toomer constructs all geographies equally.

Toomer writes that although *Cane* may be a swan song for the black rural South, "swiftly disappearing, swiftly being industrialized and urbanized by machines, motor cars, phonographs, movies. . . . 'Back to nature,' even if desirable, was no longer possible."[23] In doing so, Toomer concedes the importance of the folk to the (northern) discourse of blackness but denies its continuing plausibility as a lifestyle. He calls into question even the performability of folk life on anything more than a rhetorical level. Allowing the discourses of North and South to exist simultaneously, he demonstrates the constructedness of both, yet he insists on "progress" from the primacy of folk identity to a newer vision. Establishing a preferred performance that challenges—while not utterly denying the validity and significance of—previously "natural" ideas about race, Toomer seeks a way both to "reform" blackness and to begin to deconstruct "race" altogether. That is, by pointing out its constructedness, Toomer opens space for his own constructions. He wants to adapt the concept of "race" to new surroundings rather than adapting his surroundings to a preexisting notion of "race."

I do not wish to deny that Toomer, at many places in his work, celebrates folk spirit and folk culture. For example, in "November Cotton Flower," he uses the image of a cotton flower with "brown eyes that loved without trace of fear" (4) to symbolize the resilience of African Americans who must endure the stifling conditions represented in the poem's drought-ridden South. Indeed, as a further indication of his reverence for folk culture, he writes of himself as a "preserver" of folk culture, "I realized with deep regret, that the spirituals, meeting ridicule, would be certain to die out."[24] At such moments, Toomer again places himself and his narrator(s) in a position akin to that of Johnson's ex-colored narrator; that is, they put their "inauthentic" subject positions into service as custodians of folk culture. To equate that celebration of folk culture with the primacy of southern rural geography in the discourse of black identity, however, is to ignore the role intraracial difference plays in Toomer's work. It is the position of the narrative voice as "outsider" that drives *Cane;* it is the penetration of southern rural blackness by a well-spoken, "alien" stranger—almost in the fashion of local color writing—that makes the preservation of, and the "swan song" for, folk culture possible.[25] Like Johnson, Toomer sets up elements of folk culture as reusable building blocks that the nonfolk African American must use in an effort to reformulate, legitimate, and finally produce a "New Negro" identity that reflects the diversity of blackness in the United States. Further, while *Cane* may be a "swan song" for the rural South and its black culture, the text is also a vision of the South that runs, at times, to the dystopic.

"Esther" chronicles the ways in which intraracial color and class prejudices drive a young woman to paranoid fantasies of virgin birth and humiliation in front of (and at the hands of) the folk. With the amount of pathos that this sketch projects for a woman whom, because of her difference from a normative folk identity, the town considers "a little off, a little crazy" (24), I am hard-pressed to call "Esther" anything but a criticism of southern folk identity. Esther, a bourgeois shopkeeper's daughter, is taught the significance of race: "White folks dont divide the niggers, Esther. Be just as black as any man who has a silver dollar" (22). This focus on "egalitarian" commerce sets her apart from the African American folk

community in its emphasis on the community-building power of class—
or at least disposable income—over "race." Cash, rather than culture or
color, marks the boundaries of community, the wonderful phrase "black
as any man" deconstructing whiteness as well as blackness.

Here again Toomer sets differing discourses of identity in motion at
the same time. In this case, these discourses based on differentiating
rather than uniting prove unsatisfactory. "Race" is not deconstructed but
simply reconstructed with an eye toward class position. The chance for a
wider community afforded in a potential "Americanization" of race into
the realm of spirituality is lost. The authenticity of the "nonracial" bourgeois proves as untenable as the authenticity of the folk. Alienated from a
normative African American community through her family's insistence
on the primacy of class, Esther dreams herself back into the folk through
fantasies about Barlo, who, as a representative of the folk, is "Black. Mag-
netically so. Best cotton picker in the entire county" (23). Toomer offers
a critique of a white culture and religion that plants delusions of virgin
births in Esther's mind, but at the same time, she cannot find refuge in
folk culture. The folk forbid her from performing "their" identity, saying,
"This aint the place fer y" when—after sixteen years of watching him—
she comes to express her desire for Barlo (24). Her advance is rebuffed
with shouts of "So that's how the dictie niggers does it" (25), and Esther
is turned out from the folk in shame. Even in the face of hardship and oppression that the South represents for all African Americans regardless of
class or color, specific constructs of "race" still divide intraracially. Esther
fails to perform herself back into the folk because her audience will not accept the authenticity of her performance. Her bourgeois upbringing and
education have marked her difference from the majority of the townsfolk,
and though Esther may ultimately desire to take part in the life of that
community, her own intraracial difference appears to present an insurmountable gulf. If "race" and African American culture are not concepts
that can unite black folks, then what purpose can they serve at all?

The South is, for Toomer, as much a land of violence and cruelty as it
is the heart of a disappearing stage of black life. Nearly every poem and
vignette of section 1 is replete with images of violence. Contrary to being
a place where black identity grows in its most natural way, the South is a
location in which black identity and life may be cut down suddenly and
unnaturally. Toomer's northern black narrator describes myriad southern

scenes in which rural southern geography and its corresponding culture are figured as much as a threat to black identity as its origin. Indeed, the discourses of black identity and violence become so intertwined that their connection serves as the impetus for Toomer to deconstruct "race," denaturalize the connection between blackness and violence, and reimagine the American community as a whole. In "The Reapers," for instance, rural activities are pictured as a dangerous and bloody swinging of scythes rather than an idyllic pastoral retreat. Black is not just the color of people in this poem. Rather, it is also associated with "Black horses [that] drive a mower through the weeds" (3); the distance between human and draft animal is questioned within this geography. Tellingly, the major image of the scythes' effect is not of any harvested grain, but rather of a rat, "startled, squealing," that crosses the reapers' path as they "Blood-stained, continue cutting weeds and shade" (3). "Reapers" is an antipastoral that points out violence and lack (they harvest weeds, not grain), rather than a land of peace and plenty, revealing Toomer's ambivalence about the South even as he explores its positive aspects as the repository of a unique culture.

Further, the vignette "Blood-Burning Moon" details the death of two men, one black and the other white, competing for a woman who, in Toomer's iconography, represents much of rural southern geography. Played out in the cane fields of Georgia, "Blood-Burning Moon" explores the links between race and sexuality in the South. Bob Stone, white and racist, wants Louisa for his mistress, so "he went in as a master should and took her. None of this sneaking. . . . Hell no, his family still owned the niggers practically" (31). It appears as if slavery has been abolished here in name only; Tom Burwell, Louisa's African American lover, thinks differently, proclaiming, "white folks aint up t them tricks much nowadays. Godam better not be. Leastawise not with yo" (30). Although Tom believes that the codes of interracial behavior have changed, he is gravely mistaken. The continuation of racism after emancipation allows space for whites like Stone to assert themselves as rapists and exploiters. Tom kills Bob in a struggle over Louisa, but even this act of rebellion, this assertion of black defiance in the face of white oppression, goes primarily for naught. Tom is lynched, and the white community continues to set the boundaries of black identity. The South in *Cane* is as symbolic of death as it is a marker of wholly desirable black identity. But perhaps this is precisely Toomer's point in writing a swan song for the folk; if nothing else, it points out the visceral necessity of imagining alternative categories and authenticities. The continued use of "black" and "white" as believable, enforceable, and valid categories of social differentiation merely continues the exploitation and oppression that a racialist system of slavery set in place. African Americans are bonded now by notions of "race" rather than forced servitude, but the former is virtually as effective as the latter. And yet that bond of blackness is insufficient to create a political solidarity or ideology powerful enough to overcome white oppression.

Indeed, Toomer's South is, in terms of the narrators of the first section of *Cane,* an "other" that is at once inscrutable and terrifying. The poem "Portrait in Georgia" (27) provides an example of the geographic otherness Toomer sets up in section 1. The poem, an imagistic sort of verse, describes a white woman, but the blazon of her characteristics spells only death. I quote here in full:

> Hair—braided chestnut
>     coiled like a lyncher's rope,
> Eyes—faggots,
> Lips—old scars, or the first red blisters,
> Breath—the last sweet scent of cane,
> And her slim body, white as the ash
>     of black flesh after flame.

This portrait, labeled specifically southern by the title of the poem, is a declaration of what the South means to African Americans. It may be a place of fading customs, but the fading is being helped along by repressive violence against African Americans. The northern black man may be able to receive some sort of contact with his or "roots" by going to the South but is just as easily lynched. Given the fact of racism, the meaning of blackness is not even determined by African Americans; whiteness sets the limits of the discourse.

Further, Toomer questions the authenticity of southern identity in the poem "Conversion" by evoking an opulent African past that contrasts sharply with the vision of African Americans "Yielding to new words and a weak palabra / Of a white-faced sardonic god" (26). This poem follows immediately the vignette of "Esther" and its critique of Christianity, particularly in its "high" or "dictie" forms. Although southern folk culture may involve certain forms of religious expression, Toomer does not ever grant that religion the courtesy of a god with a capital *G*. Certainly it is the whiteness of the god that, in some respects, necessitates the speaker's refusal of it, yet the "African Guardian of Souls / Drunk with rum" is an ineffectual protector and somewhat unappealing alternative. In invoking Africa in this way, Toomer moves himself toward an assertion of his "American" race; he points out that even the southern folk are at an enormous remove from the "originary source" of black identity. He portrays the African past as one of "strange cassava," implying an otherness even one step further removed from the southern "other" who confronts the northern narrator throughout the section. Therefore, to find someone performing in a "truly" black manner, we must return to Africa, where that particular culture will not submit itself to whiteness via "grins, cries / Amen, shouts hosanna." The African past, like the folk past, is part of Toomer "the first American," but it is part of his cultural past rather than the future he is constructing for himself. In placing images of Africa and the South in the same poem, Toomer attempts to point out that neither is adequate. This poem highlights, in some significant ways, "the dialogic strategies and hybrid forms essential to the diaspora aesthetic."[26] Toomer desires to emphasize the ever-evolving sense of identity that diaspora brings rather than attempting to isolate and reify a position that can serve as a stable, authenticating marker of blackness.

Toomer goes on to make the South the "other" at another important level by figuring southern geography as female in relation to his northern male narrator(s). The South becomes even more inscrutable—indeed, more dangerous—than it might initially appear. In more than half the poems and vignettes of section 1, the main character is a woman. The male narrator(s) try to come to some deeper understanding of the South by observing its women, but a difference in gender almost always precludes any bridging of the geographic gap. In "Karintha," the narrator says that the "interest of the male, who wishes to ripen a growing thing too soon, could mean no good to her" (1). Karintha, symbol of the South, "innocently lovely as a November cotton flower" (1), is "ruined" by the masculine other. Ironically, however, Karintha becomes an exploited commodity rather than an example of viable human identity. For the narrator, "Karintha is a woman. She who carries perfect beauty, perfect as dusk when the sun goes down" (2); yet that identity is often asserted in relation to the male. Mainly through sexual interaction with men does Karintha have any meaning at all. In the first line of prose, the narrator relates that "men always wanted her" (1), placing Karintha immediately in a position of definition through masculine desire. "Young men run still to make her money. Young men go to the big cities and run the road. Young men go away to college. They all want to bring her money" (2); yet when their implicitly purchased sexual contact with her begets a child, they abandon her. As a purely sexual being, she has worth, but as a mother—with all the complex family relationships motherhood entails—her status declines. As a symbol of the South (and note that Karintha always stays in Georgia, whereas the men who desire her are quite mobile), Karintha raises problems; her gender makes her simultaneously unknowable (the men "will die not having found it out"—"it" being the "essence" of Karintha's soul) and possessable. She serves as an emblem of an identity that Toomer's male narrators cannot fathom and cannot, as evidenced by the birthing scene, perform.

By the same token, Becky, emblem of both the southern taboo and tradition of miscegenation, evokes as much male misunderstanding as anything else. She paralyzes men with fear; her otherness puts the narrator of her story (as well as other men of the area) in an almost supernatural fright. The narrator recalls:

> Through the dust we saw the bricks in a mound on the floor. Becky, if she was there, lay under them. I thought I heard a groan. Barlo, mumbling something, threw his Bible on the pile. (No one has ever touched it.) Somehow we got away. (7–8)

Becky is so alien that no one dares get near her, let alone attempt a rescue. Using the Bible as a talisman to ward off the "evil" of the desire Becky represents and the system of segregation she embodies, the narrator fails to understand the significance of the event (indeed, he blacks out from fear) but returns to town to give the "true word of it" anyway. That Becky is a white woman further complicates *Cane*'s dynamic of racial discourses in that the South becomes marked by "illicit" interracial desire (a condition amplified by "Blood-Burning Moon") that calls into question the authenticity and "purity" of social divisions along black-white lines. Toomer's figuration of the South as feminine adds to its position as the "other" of the narrative voices of section 1. The South is admired and desired because of its difference and the "secret" it seems to hold, but ultimately it tells the narrators more about what they are *not* than fixes their identity in a notion of the southern rural folk.

Ladell Payne has argued that

> in reality . . . [Toomer's vignettes of section 1] serve as commentaries on the experiences and perceptions of several young men, all of whom are trying to find an identity for themselves and to understand the world of people with whom they live. . . . In part one, Toomer presents the impressionistic responses of an outsider, a young black man much like himself, to lives and scenes set in a romantically vital rural South.[27]

In that search for identity, however, the outsider can never become an insider. The bridge between South and North, the "race consciousness" that seemingly should allow an African American narrator to connect to a southern heritage and participate in that aspect of the discourse of black identity, is too fraught with misunderstanding, danger, and death. Geographical difference represents in *Cane* part of the matrix of discourses that Toomer asks his narrators and readers to negotiate. Although folk culture is valued in the book, it is by no means a solution to problems of identity. Rather, folk culture stands as a kind of benchmark, even a historical moment, against which competing, concurrent discourses need to be assessed. Toomer's narrative voices not only fail to write themselves fully into a southern discourse of black identity; they resist it. They decline to adopt and perform "southern blackness," preferring instead to use their own "foreign" consciousness to comment on the nature of "race" and race relations.

This is not to say, however, that Toomer engaged in a romantic vision of the North. *Cane* presents the problems of urban expanses above (or, in the case of Washington, D.C., below) the Mason-Dixon line with notable candor. In describing the significance of the shift in geography between the first two sections of *Cane*, Nellie McKay writes that

> artistic tension rises from the conflict between natural human impulses and the covert violence of the man-made urban environment. In the North blacks struggle to establish identity out of the remnants of their past and the values and ideals of their newly acquired

home. . . . If black folk culture is memorable because of its connections with qualities in the natural world that could not wholly be destroyed by racial oppression, then the black urban experience is memorable because it separated the people from their basic values of the folk culture. City life initiated black people into a world of western culture, which . . . has become sterile, limiting, and destructive to the human spirit.[28]

McKay's observations on the effects of migration mark a shift away from the primacy—indeed, the "naturalness"—of southern rural identity in the early twentieth century. The preceding passage sheds light on the increasing differentiation within the category "black." The shift in geography between sections of *Cane* works in part not only in describing a new consciousness of the urban North but also in assessing the viability and desirability of that consciousness as a marker of "authentic" identity. In the second section of *Cane,* Toomer establishes the parameters of performance for a discourse of northern blackness, raising along the way the issue of how multiple "authentic" discourses might point the way toward something new. Examining intraracial difference becomes central to Toomer's de/reconstruction of racial identity in general. Geography and its connotations are simply one way of testing the ultimate viability of any type of "blackness."

McKay points to "Seventh Street," the lead prose poem of section 2, as an example of the way folk status and consciousness infused into the urban North alleviates what she views as the alienating nature of the geography. "Seventh Street" represents "the energy and determination of the black people who left the oppression of the South . . . [and who] do not easily concede defeat, even against awesome odds. . . . They transcend insurmountable hardships through the creativity of poetry and music."[29] It is via folk culture, she suggests, that black identity triumphs over urban alienation. Now, I allow that Toomer does indeed spend a good deal of time exploring urban alienation, but I also contend that the folk cannot transcend it, either. "Seventh Street" offers a rather uncomplimentary vision of certain "folk" behaviors. First off, observing this scene of the urban folk, the speaker declares that God "would duck his head in shame and call for the Judgment Day" were he black (39). A racial deity would see this conduct of his people as unacceptable, yet if we recall the drinking, womanizing, and chicanery of a "folk" character such as Barlo, there is not much difference between "folk" performance across geographic boundaries. "Seventh Street" employs images such as "bootleggers," things that "disappear in blood," and "blood-red smoke," all modifications or carryovers of the images from section 1, signaling the continuance of certain (not necessarily desirable) behaviors. Possibly, this implies that the category "folk" may be too imprecise in this new context. The term appears to function less forcefully as a specifically descriptive marker. If such performance is unrestricted by geography, Toomer intimates that "folk" may be losing some of its power to unite a variety of people and to form community, at least with respect to its situation in a specific geography. "Folk" is becoming more a generality than a culturally powerful specificity; indeed, Toomer seems to be pointing to the rise of a neourban folk that, while it shares certain traits with the "traditional" folk, also marks an increasing differentiation among concepts of African American identity.

Second, "Seventh Street" is one of only two vignettes of the second section that do not focus on an individual or group of individuals. The folk are anonymous (though flashy) "Ballooned, zooming Cadillacs"—not people at all—and whereas they were highly differentiated in section 1, Toomer here recasts the migrated southern folk as a mass. In this sense, geography makes a difference in Toomer's characterization. A northern urban folk identity may be more anonymous than its southern counterpart, but in constructing his northern folk in this fashion, Toomer further reduces their significance to a discourse of black identity. As the folk become less clearly defined, they recede from prominence within the discourse. What he sets out to examine in section 2 is the viability, and the complexity, of alternative northern black identities.

Even in poems and vignettes that several critics have called attention to as evidence that "spontaneous black life is threatened in the city by people's increasingly individualistic social ambition," Toomer does not posit the characters' particular forms of alienation as inauthentic or categorically nonblack identity.[30] Indeed, the identity of "Rhobert" or the speaker of "Beehive" is legitimized as real and authentic, even natural, consistent with Toomer's practice of engaging multiple discourses of blackness. Rhobert, for example, can be characterized as a member of the bourgeoisie who loses his soul in the race for material gain.[31] I concede that such a reading is not inconsistent with Toomer's language; after all,

Rhobert "cares not two straws as to whether he will ever see his wife and children again" (40). Still, his northern bourgeois status—as symbolized by the house—also serves to protect him from the pressures of life. He would lose his life were he to abandon his helmet/house, since life would "crush [him] the minute he pulled his head out" (40). The identity that this geography makes possible, then, is both salvation and alienation; like the folk South, the bourgeois North is far from Edenic, yet both are viable and authentic. Further, in setting up the metaphor of the diver, Toomer has made Rhobert into a pioneer, a type of courageous hero immortalized in song—"Lets open our throats, brother, and sing 'Deep River' when he goes down" (41). Rhobert is going where few of his peers have gone before, and though he pays the price in terms of his interpersonal relationships, that price does not necessarily entail an abandonment of a "natural" state of blackness. Ironically, the spiritual helps to place him in a recognizably African American context. Again, Toomer links two discourses of blackness—the folk and bourgeois "versions"—in an effort to explore the diversity of African American life. And although an emphasis like Rhobert's on material possession may indeed be anathema to Toomer's greater vision of life well lived, I want to point out that it is a criticism of urban life in general, rather than a specifically African American version of urban life. "Rhobert" suggests nothing in its title character's racial makeup that makes his descent into the depths a function of his skin color or cultural background.

Toomer reinforces this idea even further when in the poem "Beehive" (48) he creates a speaker who is part and parcel of the urban milieu. The poem begins, "Within the black hive to-nite / There swarm a million bees"; the opening lines and their driving metaphor establish the "natural" state of black urban life. Of all the images Toomer could have chosen, he selected one that relies on a state of social behavior that is anything but human. And although the poem indeed deals with the alienation of the speaker, "a drone" who wishes to "fly out past the moon / And curl forever in some far-off farmyard flower" (suggesting that rural geography has some sort of restorative powers), both geographic images—urban and rural—are taken directly from nature. In making this choice, Toomer belies the assertion that either a northern urban identity or a southern rural one is the sole natural or authentic marker of blackness. "Beehive," with its "Bees escaping to the moon, / Bees returning through the moon," implies that the discourse of black identity must be large enough to accommodate both, and though both may be present, neither is necessarily satisfactory in his wider vision of "race."

Brinkmeyer states that section 2 of *Cane* demonstrates "the anguish that arises when a person's impulses run counter to the social scheme."[32] What I find particularly noteworthy in this section of *Cane* is the complex network of social schemes that function consecutively or concurrently. It is in this web of schemes that Toomer reconstructs discourses of blackness in building toward his reinvented concept of America. In the important vignette "Theater," two characters, Dorris (a dance hall girl) and John (a bourgeois theater manager) observe each other from afar but never approach each other. The story of their attraction and desire becomes a tale of the complexities of race. "Theater" demonstrates not only that African American identity can be constructed in different, even conflicting, ways and that geography affects the performance of "race," but also that in imagining a discourse of black identity that subsumes a number of narrower discourses, "race" becomes an even more unstable, superficial marker of community. Unattainable for some in its narrow forms, authentic "race" in its wider sense is only a vaguely descriptive term rather than a practical political, social, or aesthetic tool.

With the city as a backdrop and the diversity an urban geography implies, Toomer explores intraracial class difference and the way it shapes social interaction. John is never labeled inauthentically black; on the contrary, he is described as "the mass heart of a black audience" (50). He does, however, insist on maintaining his difference from these working women by calling them "dancing ponies" (51) even while expressing his sexual desire for them.[33] Dorris reciprocates, at least in terms of a distant sexual desire, and they both worry, not about some taboo of crossing racial barriers, but rather about the social conventions of class that separate them. John muses that Dorris will consider him "dictie, educated, stuck-up" (51) while Dorris wonders "Aint I as good as him? Couldnt I have got an education if I'd wanted one?" (51). The rest of the vignette plays out their sexual fantasies about each other, but the relationship ends unconsummated. It is not the lack of race identity that keeps the two apart, but rather an adherence to codes of social class. Indeed, these codes or scripts are further emphasized by the framing metaphor of the theater itself, and although we do not find in this case the explicit references to minstrelsy coupled with theatricality that are present in Johnson, Larsen, and Schuyler, the relationship between racial identity and performance is nevertheless strongly reinforced. Further, this inability to connect with Dorris should be read not as a loss of intangible "soul" on John's part but as a commentary on the increasingly complex nature of African American identity. Toomer points out that there are factors that separate African Americans from one another, and because he does not pass judgment on either of his protagonists, he necessarily asks us to recognize variety within the discourse of "race" as well as the ways in which catholicity of performance begins to deconstruct the larger rubric describing "race."

The expansion of the discourse of black identity helps head off such stereotypical views of African American identity as Bona has of Paul: "Colored; cold. Wrong somewhere" (74). Yet even this broader notion of blackness will prove an inadequate discourse. The labels "black" and "white" are always already limiting in terms of class, geography, gender, and performance; Kerman and Eldridge point out that these categories and the baggage they carry are products of a long period of "cultural conditioning."[34] The only way to break the limiting chains of this racial discourse is to do away with "race" itself. In rejecting "race," Toomer was moving to break racism itself, since the two concepts are linked through performance; that is, racism is a specifically performed act or series of acts, behaviors, and manifested attitudes predicated on the notion of "race" and difference. Walker comments that "it is as if Toomer believed that an absence of black people assured the absence of racism itself," but Toomer also sought the absence of "white" people, too.[35] Indeed, it is not really a question in *Cane* of doing away with people having dark skin, but rather a matter of overthrowing the always already debased racial categories through which we classify one another. Only by refusing and refiguring prevailing notions of "race" can one build toward a liberating coalition politics and aesthetics.

Of course, because one does not believe in "race" in an intellectual sense does not mean there is no such thing as racism, but as a linguistic and artistic endeavor, *Cane*'s refigurations of "race" are indeed a step toward the reformation of "behavior which consists in the display of contempt or aggressiveness toward other people on account of physical differences."[36] Toomer chips away at the links between language and performance; he moves to reimagine a community where language is stripped of its specifically "racial" meaning, thereby rendering actions in accordance with that language difficult, if not impossible. If *Cane* never quite gives us a glimpse of Toomer's New America, it is at least instructive in its attempts to dismantle the "old" one.

Because Toomer never quite breaks free from established notions of "race" in *Cane,* geographic location and background can lead to a state of (in)authenticity, the pull between the desire to write or act oneself into the folk-centered discourse and the recognition that such a discourse is inadequate to describe certain African American subject positions, consequently becoming a suspect marker of community, culture, and tradition. Section 3 of *Cane,* the short story–drama "Kabnis," takes this (in)authenticity as its central theme. Aside from being perhaps the most discussed portion of Toomer's work, "Kabnis" has intrigued critics because of Toomer's proclamation that "Kabnis is *ME*."[37] But whatever similarities "Kabnis" may share with Toomer's own biography, the piece deserves close scrutiny in its own right. Although full-length chapters and articles have been dedicated to the story's explication, I shall take here a more narrow view to see how intraracial difference is played out in terms of geography.[38]

Ralph Kabnis comes to the South as an urban bourgeois northerner to teach school. The story opens with Kabnis's geographical apprehension— "If I could feel that I came to the South to face it" (81)—and his cursing of his rural circumstances, eventually wringing the neck of a chicken in the next room (a scene not as easily played out in the urban North). Geography serves as a marker of alienation and discontent. Unhappy with his circumstance, feeling himself the outsider, Kabnis takes vengeance on a South to which he is not party, attempting to exorcise the power it seems to exert on his psyche. From the outset, geography is linked inextricably with identity, and one must give credence to the possibility that in attempting to "face the South," Kabnis searches for the "former strengths of the folk culture [lost] by the city-bred generations of black people."[39] "Kabnis" could deal centrally with a search for identity based on a shift in geography. That would assume, however, that geographic difference can ultimately be overcome; the North and its culture must give in to southern culture if that lost identity is to be reclaimed.

"Kabnis" certainly seems to move in this direction, though haltingly so, with the introduction of Halsey, African American blacksmith and friend to Kabnis. The narrator describes Halsey's home as "middle-class" but also asserts that "there is a seediness about it" (85). This is not the image of the ultraclean, very proper, northern bourgeois household of a Mrs. Pribby in "Box Seat"; the South marks a difference among even the black bourgeoisie, but the dialogue suggests that such a gap can be bridged. Halsey, Kabnis, and Layman discuss how Kabnis "aint like most northern niggers. . . . Aint a thing stuck up about him" (86). And Kabnis adds that "theres lots of northern exaggeration about the South. . . . Things are not half bad, as one could easily figure out for himself without ever crossing the Mason and Dixon line: all these people wouldn't stay down here, especially the rich, the ones that could easily leave, if conditions were so mighty bad" (87). Neither Kabnis nor his southern companions perform "race" in the ways in which they have learned it "should" be played with respect to geographic difference. It is in this moment of well-behaved mutual admiration that a "race consciousness" is born; the three go on to agree that a "nigger's a nigger down this way" (87), though the similarity they are positing is actually in the eyes of whites rather than an intraracial feeling of brotherhood. As Judith Butler might suggest, this performance of racial solidarity is "but a ritualized production, a ritual reproduced under and through constraint, under and through the force of prohibition and taboo, with the threat of ostracism and even death controlling and compelling the shape of the production."[40] These characters in "Kabnis" seize this moment to gather together in the face of oppression, creating a tenuous solidarity in the face of limiting and limited roles prescribed on the basis of race and geography.

It does not take long, despite talk of "good conditions" and the absurdity of regional chauvinism, for intraracial geographic-cultural difference to surface, not merely in a superficial way, but so as to indicate a more deep-seated distinction between North and South. Not only does Kabnis find certain southern cultural practices repugnant—"Couldnt stand the shouting, and thats a fact," he says of a southern religious service (89)— but the brick that crashes through Halsey's parlor window bearing the message "You northn nigger, its time fer y t leave" (90), attests to the apparent irreconcilability of North and South. No matter for whom the brick was intended (Kabnis or not) or who threw it (white or black) the threat serves to point out at least the perceived incompatibility of North and South. And when perception borders on bodily harm, the construction of geographic difference takes on a real status. Although a northerner's performance of "race" is not necessarily antithetical to the African American's "place" in the South, constructed notions of geographic difference are so threatening as to induce both inter- and intraracial xenophobia.

Despite his condemnation of school superintendent Hanby, whom Kabnis describes as a pretentious assimilationist who "lets it be known that his ideas are those of the best New England tradition" (93), Kabnis is such a foreigner to the South that he can never really surmount the geographic barriers facing him. Terrified by the brick intended for another man, and fired from his job, Kabnis becomes even more alienated from his southern surroundings, prompting Layman to declare that "teaching in th South aint th thing fer y. Nassur. You ought t be way back up North" (97). Obviously, Kabnis has not yet learned the proper performance of southern blackness; the North is to serve as his refuge, his touchstone to his own identity. Yet Kabnis stays on, perhaps to confront the South in hopes of expanding his own notion of personal identity, working in Halsey's shop.

Indeed, Kabnis moves even further "south" than he has previously been located, living in Halsey's cellar, also known as "the Hole."[41] His decision to remain in Georgia and his new position as a manual-labor apprentice bring him, in some respects, even closer to the position of the southern folk. *Cane*'s final scene, however, insists on the maintenance of intraracial difference. Kabnis winds up denouncing Father John, symbol of the South and folk history, as an "old black fakir" (116). And although there is some indication that Kabnis does indeed acknowledge the significance of the folk and southern folk history, the piece ends with Kabnis emerging from the Hole—and thereby the South—without ever really having embraced the folk or modeled himself on them. Kabnis may develop a new appreciation of the difference geography makes, but he is not basically transformed by his journey. Understanding the past, one of the major tenets of developing a "race consciousness," does not automatically trigger some sort of "natural" code of conduct; it does not give the script to "authentic" racial performance. That we know history does not mean that we become part of a cultural teleology. A recognition of the past is not a recipe for the future. So Kabnis's identity as an alien remains intact, the light shining through the cellar window as symbolic of Carrie K. and Father John's new understanding of Kabnis as Kabnis's acceptance of the South. Identity is not discovered by traversing geographic boundaries, for it is, in Kabnis, already solidly in place. An appreciation of difference is the best that can be hoped for, and indeed that is what *Cane* achieves.

Toomer's northern characters all ultimately fail to write, work, teach, preach, or believe themselves into the discourse that privileges the southern rural folk. What some of them successfully achieve, however, is the ability to see intraracial difference and grant it a place. They become, in some respect, content with an (in)authenticity with regard to folk culture; to be truly folk is not the only way to be racial. Geography may help determine consciousness, but there needs to be room for more than one type of consciousness in the discourse of black identity. And yet in the long run, Toomer begins to question the adequacy of any discourse of black identity at all, at least in terms of its geographical component. In writing a swan song for the South, Toomer also implicitly writes a swan song for the North. Setting itself apart by pointing to its converse, one geography defines the other. And when one of these geographies begins to "fade away," part of the support structure for racial categorization falls away with it. Without a solid geographic point of reference, "race" becomes an even more difficult and unstable distinction to employ. As Kabnis learns, we need to overcome narrowness of definition. If these two opposites no longer adequately define the African American condition, we must begin to search for new terms to describe performances that we previously attributed to the intersections of "race" and geography. In describing complexity, we need to eschew simplicity of terminology; the language of racialist discourse, loaded as it is with class, gender, and geographic assumptions, is an increasingly unacceptable medium of expression. Anticipating Schuyler and his works, Toomer begins to express dissatisfaction not so much with *being* "racial" (after all, he is an American, as vague as that may seem) but with the limits placed on us by continuing to uphold and function under traditional notions of "race."

Further, if Toomer is to be criticized, with respect to either *Cane* or any of his other work, for a failure to produce a specific and concrete identity as an alternative to dismantled blackness, we might do well to recall some of Butler's observations on identity politics and the place of the subject. She writes that the "insistence on coherent identity as a point of departure presumes that what the 'subject' is is already known, already fixed. . . . But if that very subject produces its coherence at the cost of its complexity, the crossing of identifications of which it is itself composed, then that subject forecloses the kinds of contestatory connections that might democratize the field of its own operation."[42] It is, perhaps, the very incoherence of identity in Toomer that is potentially most liberating, and as we shall see in the next chapter on Nella Larsen, it is the insistence on the simplification and coherence of subject positions that can prove most deadly.

# A Clash of Birthrights: Nella Larsen, the Feminine, and African American Identity

In the previous chapters, I have spoken of gender more in terms of "gendering" than as a construct of personal identity; that is, I have spent more effort describing the ways in which gender is employed as a trope invoking a sense of difference within the discourse of black identity than on the mechanisms by which gender and its own discourses, as a marker of one's individuality, affect one's position within the discourse of black identity itself. "Race" is a construct supported by an elaborate code of signs and signifiers, but so, too, is "gender." When James Weldon Johnson and Jean Toomer gender the South feminine, to what extent are they subordinating the construct of gender to the construct of race, and what are the consequences of doing so? To what extent do such writers rely on notions of "authentic" womanhood and manhood to build an "authentic" race? Must one construct always be ancillary to the other? Must one be either "truly" racial or "true" to one's gender, or can one be both?

These questions, so crudely put here, Nella Larsen

both poses and seeks to answer in her novel *Quicksand* (1928). Written at the height of the Harlem Renaissance, *Quicksand* explores the possibilities of being black *and* female simultaneously. It examines the discourse of blackness as it functions in conjunction and at cross-purposes with the discourse of womanhood.[1] Larsen addresses the gendering of racial authenticity—and the racializing of gender authenticity—by presenting us with an extended study of female characters rather than Toomeresque sketches; she points to the intersections of race and gender and, in doing so, demonstrates the ways in which the discourse of black identity often restricts the range of possible female identity in maintaining some standard of the "authentic." This is not to say that the term "gender" is synonymous with "female"; to make such an assertion would be not more accurate than to equate "race" solely with "blackness." Helga Crane's particular situation, however, deals with the especially volatile nexus of blackness *and* femininity, as well as geographical location/migration and class status. Certainly, these intersections are expressed by Toomer as well, yet in *Quicksand* the presence of a central feminine consciousness adds further complexity to an analysis of the construction of subject positions, since the feminine represents still another layer of oppression and invisibility to be negotiated. Rather than allowing the feminine to be simply manipulated as a convenient marker to illuminate the "authentically" black and masculine (as in Toomer), Larsen attempts to give a distinct and independent voice to the feminine, thereby bringing the discussion of "race" to an even more complex level.

We might return for a moment to Judith Butler's important theorization of multiple identifications within the single subject:

> To prescribe an exclusive identification for a multiply constituted subject, as every subject is, is to enforce a reduction and a paralysis. . . . And here it is not simply a matter of honoring the subject as a plurality of identifications, for these identifications are invariably imbricated in one another, the vehicle for one another: a gender identification can be made in order to repudiate or participate in a race identification; what counts as "ethnicity" frames and eroticizes sexuality, or can itself be a sexual marking. This implies that it is not a matter of relating race and sexuality and gender, as if they were fully separable axes of power.[2]

Part of what I shall be discussing in this chapter on *Quicksand* are the possibilities, as Larsen sees them, for the African American woman to maintain and develop multiple simultaneous identifications. What are the mechanisms that might allow one to do so? What are the performative codes that both enable and limit such a complex discursive performance? Given the prevailing constructs of "race" and gender, is such a multiple and complex series of identifications possible, and what are the consequences of attempting to challenge normative scripts of performance? Ultimately, Larsen's protagonist is forced to choose a "coherent" identity that must necessarily, given the prevailing discourses of race and gender, lead her to her doom. Larsen astutely contrasts the drive for a single, naturalized authenticity of identity, one that recalls the lament for lost birthrights at the end of *The Autobiography of an Ex-Colored Man*, with a vision of possible multiple, simultaneous, and performative subject positions.

Larsen begins this engagement with the "authentic" from the outset of her novel. She quotes Langston Hughes's "Cross" as the epigraph but, rather than deeming the poem exemplary of her subject, seizes on its construction of difference, recasting the famous poem in such a way as to question the discourse of black identity in which Hughes participates. Hughes's poem sets up a framework for identity that Larsen's protagonist Helga Crane will struggle against and undermine throughout *Quicksand*. Larsen quotes only the last stanza of "Cross," but if we are to understand its full significance in the novel, we need to look at the entire text of the poem:

> My old man's a white old man
> And my old mother's black
> If I ever cursed my white old man
> I take my curses back.
>
> If I ever cursed my black old mother
> And wished she were in hell,
> I'm sorry for that evil wish
> And now I wish her well.
>
> My old man died in a fine big house.
> My ma died in a shack.
> I wonder where I'm gonna die,
> Being neither white nor black? [3]

Deborah McDowell, in her introduction to the American Women Writers Series edition of *Quicksand,* points out that "the argument that Helga's is a story of the 'tragic mulatto' is clearly supported by the novel's epigraph. . . . [but] in focusing on the problems of the 'tragic mulatto,' readers miss the more urgent problem of female sexual identity which Larsen tried to explore."[4] If we recall *The Autobiography of an Ex-Colored Man,* as well as numerous other texts in the American literary tradition, we are aware that the issue of mulattoism and the figure of the mulatto can have significant bearing on the discourse of black identity. McDowell is correct in asserting the primacy of sexual identity in Larsen's text. Larsen's invocation of "Cross" questions the roles of gender and class in the discourse of black identity; more than merely placing *Quicksand* within some tradition of "tragic mulatto" fiction, the epigraph provides Larsen with a starting point from which to begin rewriting a particular gendered discourse of black identity.

If we can look beyond the enticing (and illuminating in its own right) interpretation of "Cross" as "tragic mulatto" poem, we can observe that Hughes enters into a discourse of black identity similar to the ones I have suggested that Johnson and Toomer both attempt to engage and reform. Hughes genders blackness as feminine, the mother being the only "truly" black character in the poem. Blackness is working-class, if not underclass ("ma died in a shack"), whereas whiteness is at least bourgeois ("a fine big house"). What Hughes invokes is a discourse of black identity that asserts the feminine underclass as a locus of black authenticity.[5] The speaker is an (in)authentic mixture of races, (in)authentic in the sense that a one-drop racial code makes her or him, indeed, black; yet the speaker herself or himself struggles to come to terms with this genetic "impurity" and the socioeconomic determinism that "race" can imply in a color-conscious America. The speaker is left, in this poem, with an open destiny; in wondering "where I'm gonna die," he or she views at least the possibility of developing a consciousness and performing an identity in such a way that he or she can acquire some modicum of control over that final resting place. (In)authenticity apparently functions as a realm of possibility, and not one of determinism. That is, the poem's speaker, through the assertion of possible alternative (and perhaps even subversive) identity positions, may influence the direction of life's course depending on which discourse of "race" he or she decides to embrace.

This space for maneuver is, to be sure, part of the convention of the "tragic mulatto," and the speaker's dilemma is designed, to some extent, "to invoke sympathy in the reader."[6] That is, the speaker is cast as being "orphaned" in a world between races. But aware of the (in)authenticity of the mulatto figure, Larsen attempts to reinsert her or him into the discourse of black identity in such fashion as to place a new emphasis on the performative within that discourse. She seeks to offer alternative and intersecting discourses of identity that complicate "race" and its related literary conventions as easily knowable categories.

Larsen switches the premises of Hughes's discourse in an attempt to open up a range of possible black subjectivities. In *Quicksand*, Helga's "old man" is black, and her mother white; although this may seem insignificant at first glance, Larsen's attention to the influence of sexuality on racial categorization makes the choice important. The speaker of "Cross" wonders about his or her final class status; Helga is, for most of *Quicksand* at least, aggressively bourgeois in many of her tastes and attitudes. The question is not so much "where" she will die but, initially, how she will achieve the "fine, big house." Finally, Hughes makes it explicit that the speaker is racially (in)authentic; she or he is caught between constructions of blackness and whiteness, resulting in Hughes's "tragic" dilemma. For Larsen, this is never the case. At no point in *Quicksand* does Helga ever consider herself white. Passing is never an option in this novel; blackness is always assumed. In making this a distinctive part of her novel, Larsen attempts to move beyond the dead end of tragic mulattoism toward a more complex discourse of black identity. In engaging "Cross," Larsen stakes a territory within the aesthetics and politics of Harlem Renaissance identity discourse and reexamines the possibility of multiple African American subject positions;[7] as Ann E. Hostetler points out, "Helga attempts to create a spectrum rather than an opposition" in terms of African American identity.[8] Like Johnson and Toomer before her, Larsen tries to break from prescriptive notions of blackness, but as we shall see, gender makes her attempt at creating a viable alternative African American subject position all the more difficult.

In considering *Quicksand,* one could trace much of its structure to the kind of exploration of alternative class and geographic positions undertaken by Toomer and Johnson. While Larsen critiques bourgeois materialism and the "uplift" mentality of the black middle class, she also finds fault with folk culture. Black "society" may be stifling in its "self-righteousness and intolerant dislike of difference,"[9] but certain aspects of folk culture, such as the religion symbolized by Pleasant Green, are merely "shields from the cruel light of unbearable reality" (126). And while there is nothing inherently damning about "protection" from an oppressive hegemony, Larsen seems to suggest that this is as much a "world of make-believe" as that of E. Franklin Frazier's bourgeoisie. As a result of this ambivalence toward the desirability (and even viability) of folk identity, several critics have seized on factors that distance Helga from folk status and have pointed to the ways in which Helga participates in a "race consciousness" that hypocritically serves as a "proclamation of the undiluted good of all things Negro which disguised a disdain, contempt, and amusement for the *actual* culture and behavior of the majority of black people."[10] Indeed, much like Johnson's ex-colored man, Helga, although she despises members of the folk, ultimately relies on the concept of "folk" for establishing an African American identity. Much of these characters' ambivalence about their identities comes from the gulf between their own lived experiences and concepts of blackness deriving from a demographically broader slice of black American life around which a sense of African American community is often built. As Hazel Carby implies, we tend to see Helga as a character out of the mainstream, uninvolved—at least in some respects—with the "actualities" of African American culture, a concept we have already seen Stuart Hall critique (see chapter 3). In reconstructing the "reality of race," however, we need to watch where we draw the boundaries between authentic and inauthentic.

Certainly, a reading of Larsen as a chronicler of middle-class folly is not without its merits, but too strict an adherence to such a reading risks advocating a class-based notion of African American identity that, with regard to *Quicksand,* is dubious at best. Lillie P. Howard, for example, writes that "because [Helga] cannot reconcile herself to the reality of her race . . . [she] is driven toward a materialism which masks the essence of herself."[11] Howard insists on the diametric opposition of blackness and material wealth (not to mention the possibly problematic, but very explicit, insistence on "essence"), but Larsen, I think, is more reluctant to make such class-race links. Anne Grey may serve as an example of hypocrisy in the New Negro Movement, the desire of certain African Americans to be white—for example, Larsen's ironic comment that Anne "honestly thought she believed" (48) in racial equality—while espousing the virtues of blackness and reveling in an "orgy of protest" (48). Indeed, the name "Grey" suggests being caught between black and white, but Helga herself—and we must keep in mind that this is Helga's story—is, as Hostetler points out, one of the "black characters who are every bit as capable as whites of choosing and enjoying 'nice things.'"[12] Larsen hesitates to make such a one-to-one correlation between racial identity and class position, particularly since she chooses Hughes's "Cross" as a foil for her own work. As Helga indulges her bourgeois tastes for clothes, furnishings, and other material goods, Larsen never for a moment casts doubt on Helga's racial categorization. Helga is always a black woman, although she does not necessarily accept her prescribed roles within the various racial communities she encounters.

Yet even as Larsen refuses to move Helga into a nonblack racial classification, she creates in this character an ambivalence toward possible African American subject positions. Helga becomes engaged in a struggle of internal identification that serves as a device by which Larsen places into view the ways in which notions of blackness are often an "imperfect fit" for some African Americans and the kinds of dilemmas that may cause. While maintaining "black" as a real and significant category of American identity, Larsen allows her character Helga to further interrogate exactly what underlies this notion of "race." Moreover, Larsen complicates notions of possible subjectivities by exposing the factor of affective response in the process of defining one's self. Helga is not motivated strictly by political, ideological, or moral considerations, but she also has to struggle with questions of taste and emotion. After she has spent some time in Harlem, the narrator of *Quicksand* says about Helga: "Not only did the crowds of nameless folk on the street annoy her, she began also actually to dislike her friends" (48). The narrator explains that Helga feels "estrangement and isolation" (47). On the one hand, the manners and life of the folk, their "grinning faces and . . . easy laughter" (48), put her off. Far from the gentility of Naxos, the folk come to represent an anonymous, unremarkable life that Helga attempts to elude. For her the members of the folk are an undifferentiated mass that represents a threat to her own desire for individuality.[13] Their behavior and demeanor, while hardly negative in themselves, still represent the "street," which Helga wants to avoid and finds aesthetically unpleasing. On the other hand, she dislikes her drawing-room companions because they are "obsessed by the race problem" (48). In throwing themselves (at least rhetorically) into those issues, they cast their stated sympathies, if not their actions, with the folk world Helga is looking to evade, elevating the folk to the position of Locke's vanguard. Certainly the black bourgeoisie must also confront racism in their daily lives, but it is this displacement of the "race problem" onto the folk that Helga appears to find vexing. Helga seeks a discourse that allows her to be black and middle-class without having to profess "uplift." The morality of her wish may be suspect, but the moral imperatives of racial identity are part of what she is trying to struggle against.

Helga can accept the cultural life of neither bourgeoisie nor folk. Her critique of "faux" middle-class authenticity is balanced by her distaste for the "essential" folk. In making such a statement, Larsen asks her readers to complicate their notions of black identity. African American by virtue of a racist, one-drop hegemony (and unwilling or unable to pass), Helga has her identity determined by the state and American racialist tradition, yet she must still seek community and a sense of personal, self-defined identity among those who are also always already determined. Internal and communal identity does not necessarily follow from external categorization. In this respect, blackness is more than adherence to one class position or another even though class may not even be an issue in "white" eyes. That is, within a racist society, melanin alone often proves sufficient to blur class distinctions; but merely because Helga is classified as African American by the white-dominated system does not mean she "feels herself" or "behaves" in an easily categorized African American manner. Both bourgeoisie and folk can prove unsatisfactory as markers of blackness if they link themselves to a conception of "race" that provides for an essential unity of blackness. Hegemony does this in its own right, and Helga is searching for a way to subvert that discourse.

At least in Helga Crane's case, class alone is insufficient to establish a stable black self. Helga can go from snobbish Naxos to the folk life with Pleasant Green, but those shifts in class position do not necessarily provide her with the key to establishing a normative or even stable sense of identity. That she can live among Naxos uplifters, Harlem New Negroes, Danes, and the southern folk, and adapt to their lifestyles or become—with some effort, since it often takes a while to "get it right"—part of their community does not mean she is "one of them." Since identity is at least partially, from Larsen's perspective, performative, Helga has the option of repeating the various codes of these communities in such a way as to "fit in," but she refuses to do so as she continues her quest for a community that allows her to realize all the various, and sometimes conflicting, aspects of her self-perceived identity. Larsen suggests that Helga can perform various types of class identity, but either settling on one or invoking another is no guarantee of finding stability within the discourse of black identity.

The same is true of geography in *Quicksand*, a book that is more of a journey through various "regions of race" than Toomer's *Cane*. Hostetler describes Helga's journey as one dictated by "the narrowness of place as described by race in the United States of the 1920's." [14] That is, given oppression and segregation, there are only a limited number of geographic positions available to African Americans. Within those geographies, however, expectations of a normative black identity may vary. Helga journeys from South to North to Europe back to New York and to the South again. In each locale, she meets with different expectations of black identity and encounters various archetypal people who embody some particular version of normative African American identity. Further, her geographic wanderings, like those of Toomer's narrator, are closely connected with changes in class status, making apparent the performability and instability of African American identity. As Helga inserts herself into various moments of the discourse of black identity, she begins to discover just how malleable identity can be.

To give a summary of Helga Crane's several class- and geography-based classifications, I start before the novel even begins. Helga is born into a northern, black, nonbourgeois ("in a Chicago slum" [21]) geography that carries with it certain markers of who she "should be"; she is the daughter of a black father and a white mother who disowns her. Helga further demonstrates the inability of several discourses of identity to find a place for her, since the story of her origin, "dealing as it did with race intermingling and possibly adultery, was definitely beyond discussion" (39). Ironically, the "unspeakable" act is itself written on Helga's body, suggesting an almost ludicrous inability of certain bourgeois racial discourses to, in fact, deal with the complexities of racial and sexual interactions. Helga's mother eventually marries a financially comfortable white man, but Helga is not accepted into the white bourgeoisie because of her blackness. At Naxos, however, Helga joins the African American southern bourgeoisie, characterized in its difference from the folk by the suppression of "enthusiasm [and] spontaneity" and the promotion of "self-satisfaction" (5). Fleeing Naxos, she makes her next extended geographic stop in Harlem as a sometimes participant in, but mostly observer of, a fictionalized middle-class New Negro Movement. Her trip to Europe marks another sojourn among the white bourgeoisie, and the novel ends with Helga living among the southern rural folk as a woman who "don' nebah complain an' frets no mo'e" (126) about the difficult circumstances in her life. Like Toomer's multiple characters and narrators, Helga Crane attempts to come to some understanding of her own identity by inserting herself into different class and geographic positions within the discourse of black identity.

In having Helga pursue these multiple positions, Larsen calls to mind James Weldon Johnson's narrator in *The Autobiography of an Ex-Colored Man* and his lifelong journey. Both Helga and Johnson's narrator move between folk and bourgeoisie, North and South, Europe and the United States. Johnson's narrator, however, ends his tale by passing and bemoaning the loss of his "birthright"; Helga Crane, on the other hand, ends up in the heart of the African American folk and appears to be equally, if not more, damned than the ex-colored man. Is Larsen's ending an ironic rewriting of the African American's "birthright" as a deserved, desired, and stable life among the folk? Hazel Carby is correct in asserting that Larsen deliberately "refused a romantic evocation of the folk." [15] Paula Giddings notes that Helga's foray into the rural South represents just one more instance of her "searching for her place" within the discourse of black identity. [16] That is, Helga's foray into a life among the folk with the ironically named Pleasant Green does not serve as the ultimate solution of identity trouble to a woman who has been alienated from her "birthright" of a normative or stable black identity. As Larsen constructs the situation, Helga's geographic wanderings demonstrate that geography alone, or even its conjunction with class position, is insufficient to lend one a sense of complete, natural, or essential identity. In contrast to Johnson's and Toomer's narrators who see, rightly or wrongly, the folk (or contact with the folk culture) as essential to their being, Helga Crane is ultimately damned by this contact. Indeed, there is a further complication of "race" in this comparison: the intersection of race and sexuality. Johnson's narrator flees the southern folk after witnessing a lynching, a response to black male sexuality. Helga does not escape the southern folk after her contact with them, and her sexuality, as I shall demonstrate later, proves to be her death warrant. Both Johnson's narrator and Helga are categorized in potentially fatal ways because the discourse of "race" also takes into account the sexualized body. In light of this factor, it becomes even more difficult for one to "perform" oneself out of a particular discourse without having to disregard the body itself. Whereas Johnson's narrator does, in fact, succeed in recasting the discourse of "race" written on his body, Helga has a more arduous task.

Larsen's evocation of the continuing failure of Helga to find a "natural" niche in the discourse of black identity marks a deepening in the understanding of the workings of African American identity in creative literature. Helga serves notice to the student of African American letters that it is not enough to posit blackness as a function of the rural South or urban North, or to say that the black bourgeoisie is simply as "authentic" as the folk. Further, authentic black identity, when one considers the great complexity of Larsen's *Quicksand,* cannot be reduced simply to tropes such as "passing" or the "tragic mulatto/a." Cheryl Wall argues that the "tragedy of these mulattoes is the impossibility of self-definition. Larsen's protagonists assume false identities that ensure social survival but result in psychological suicide. In one way or another, they all 'pass.'" [17]

In many senses, Helga does, in fact, assume "false" identities or at least participate in performances that are false in terms of her desires, experiences, and self-image. But the problems Helga Crane raises are more than personal character flaws neatly determined by biological circumstance. Rather, they go to the heart of the ways in which we define racial identity itself. Which identity could provide psychological salvation? Can a stabilized notion of identity even provide that salvation at all? There are only limited options from which to choose, but none of them appears acceptable in light of the way Helga continually complicates the politics of identity. What Helga Crane reminds us is that there is, indeed, the possibility of multiple authentic subject positions vis-à-vis race, but that not everyone has equal access to those positions, nor is any one position necessarily the most desirable. Implicit in Larsen's novel is a suggestion that in choosing and maintaining one "stable" subject position, the complex person runs the risk of effectively amputating certain interests and desires for the sake of conformity. This, it seems to me, calls into question the desirability of many kinds of rigid, stable self-definitions, yet at the same time, it points out the kinds of difficulties one faces in refusing to accept paradigmatic performances of subject positions.

For Helga Crane, the "impossibility of self-definition" is not a question of mixed parentage but rather a result of her inability to perform/write herself into a normative discourse of black identity because of the complex relationships between her gender and class and geographical origins. Larsen questions the ways in which authentic black identity is constructed by pointing out that such racial identity is contingent on gender identity. Racial authenticity becomes a function of which gender roles a person assumes. Indeed, I have already pointed to the ways in which Johnson and Toomer employ gender in (re)writing discourses of black identity, but Larsen is significant because she moves beyond the use of gender as a mere literary trope. Gender and its construction become factors that define black identity rather than metaphors describing blackness. The feminine and masculine are as much performable subject positions as blackness and whiteness, and for Helga, the double performance of black womanhood is no easy feat. Whereas Toomer's narrators rarely have to think about how their masculinity is performed (since it is a more naturalized type of subject position, much like whiteness is with respect to blackness), Helga is continually faced with the conscious need—and demand—to balance and reconcile both race and gender. Larsen brings out aspects of the race-gender interrelationship that Toomer and Johnson either silence or inadequately express. These male writers and the male protagonists can move toward, if not actually discover, an authentic African American identity partially because they have the power in their narratives to control the feminine. In the search for their birthright of blackness, they can possess women, write them in and out of the text at will. Larsen, in contrast, gives us Helga Crane, who must struggle against such possession by male characters in an effort to arrive at satisfactory notions of *both* gender *and* racial identity. Indeed, in trying to assert control over her own body and resist roles ascribed to her by a patriarchal and racist hegemony, Helga discovers her quicksand, a clash of birthrights between womanhood and blackness, a determining discourse of black womanhood that, in its own right, pits one identity against the other.

Although I have already questioned the notion of a "birthright" as a natural or essential portion of a person's identity (see chapter 2), it might prove useful to examine the concept here briefly because it is a term that Larsen uses, though perhaps ironically, in *Quicksand*. During Helga's initial sojourn in Harlem, she reflects, when considering white Americans on the street, on "sinister folk . . . who had stolen her birthright" (45). Clearly, the sentiment is directed at the pernicious effects of racism; by channeling her anger at "sinister" whiteness, Helga comments on an American culture in which skin color sets the parameters of perception, behavior, and accomplishment. In addition to being an example of the way Helga—though mulatto and light skinned—is inscribed in America's racial discourse, the passage suggests the way in which blackness is constructed as non-self-defining in racist discourse. That is, whiteness is dependent on a blackness that can be subordinated—a blackness that, as the constructed "other," has its number of possible subject positions limited— by the "natural" superiority of whiteness. Further, such a description has resonances for the feminine, too, in that sexist discourse often constructs the feminine as non-self-defining. A stolen birthright implies a lack of control over one's own destiny, a lack of voice in a chorus of competing interests. Yet the particular construction of a "birthright" will have a profound effect on the shaping of the future; differently conceived birthrights will lead to different ends.

Of course, true to Larsen's talent for ambiguity, one can never be quite sure what this birthright is: the right to live independently without reliance on others for her livelihood, equal rights and status under the law, the ability to acknowledge her mixed racial heritage without fear or shame, some other right, all of these rights, or some combination of them. Indeed, it is indicative of Helga Crane's search for a stable notion of identity that that birthright is a slippery concept; with an identity so malleable and mercurial, it is difficult to nail down exactly what Helga was "born" to do or be. Nevertheless, the use of the term suggests that in the construction of a discourse of identity, we come to think of certain aspects of identity as basic, fundamental, and requisite. These are things bestowed on us simply by virtue of being, and to lose them is, in some way, to be stripped of some integral part of the self.

To define one's birthright, whether it is indeed a natural essence or a constructed phenomenon, gives one the power, at least to a certain extent, to shape one's own identity. Helga Crane, as an African American woman, has the doubly difficult task of coming to terms with not only two aspects of identity, blackness and femininity, but also two marginalized aspects of identity. She must continually struggle against both patriarchal and racial oppression, often confronting them in concert. Although racism is not always patriarchal, a combination of these two repressive forces frequently shapes Helga's identity. In moving toward self-definition, Helga regularly has to make choices: to fight patriarchy, to fight racism, or to fight both simultaneously. What she discovers, however, is that the drives toward race and gender identification often conflict, requiring one aspect of her identity to be subordinated to another. Sometimes, as in Europe, she must internalize racism to perform her identity as a particular type of (semi-)independent woman; at other times, Helga submits to patriarchy in an effort to avoid being a person "who do[es] not have a commitment to a racial collective" in a fight against the American racial caste system.[18] As Helga Crane discovers, though, the discourse that has as its birthright the overriding solidarity of race comes directly into conflict with her status as an independent, self-defining woman.

Priscilla Ramsey states that Larsen "escalates her attack on black middle-class social life of her era by creating women who are forced into lives of limitation, ennui and boredom."[19] Embedded within that statement is an observation of the way in which gender must be subordinated to race in certain discourses of blackness. Class and race parameters of community prescribe the boundaries of the feminine. And although Helga's life is possibly less one of limitation, boredom, and ennui as a member of the Harlem bourgeoisie than it is as Mrs. Pleasant Green, to retain the birthrights of blackness within a folk context, Helga must necessarily put aside the independence that class and geography afforded her in her pursuit of female self-definition. Although she is by no means an equal to men within bourgeois society, Helga still comes closer to realizing an independence there than among the southern folk, who are "bound together through [their] allegiance to the black preacher . . . who appeared as an Old Testament patriarch."[20] The language of that phrase alone calls into question the desirability of a folk identity aimed at creating a community on the basis of race; women are "bound" to African American community through a dominating "patriarch."

This construction stands in contrast to several moments in Helga's bourgeois existence. At Naxos, for example, Dr. Anderson, the principal, offers Helga a "leadership" position as the "conscience" of the institution in an attempt to dissuade her from leaving; he asks, "And don't you think it might help cure us, to have someone who doesn't approve of these [behaviors at Naxos] stay with us? Even if only one person?" (19). Although it is not an officially sanctioned position of power, Helga is extended a position of "moral" leadership. Her power to shape the community from a feminine subject position is acknowledged. Such a recognition marks a substantial difference from her place among the folk, where when Helga attempts to use her position as the patriarch's wife to promote a kind of uplift, she meets stiff resistance. Helga hopes to "subdue the cleanly scrubbed ugliness of her own surroundings to soft inoffensive beauty, and to help the other women do likewise . . . [and] to try to interest the women in what she considered more appropriate clothing and inexpensive ways of improving their homes" (119). For these efforts, however, she is characterized by the folk as "dat uppity, meddlin' No'then'nah" married to their patriarch, who "would 'a done bettah to a ma'ied Clementine Richards" (119), a woman from the folk who better knows her position within that community. Helga's class and geographic background inscribes her notion of "women's work" in such a way that places her outside the prevailing notion of femininity. Within the matrix of class, geography, and gender, Helga finds her actions judged through a complex series of assumptions that almost always challenge her ideal expectation for a stable subject position.

This quicksand of birthrights ultimately exposes the ways in which communities based on race and class use hierarchies of gender to perpetuate themselves. As a member of the bourgeoisie, Helga can obtain "the things that money could give, leisure, attention, beautiful surroundings" (67), but she herself becomes an object within that system of discourse. By the same token, in writing her into the folk discourse of blackness, Larsen also has Helga give up her birthrights as a woman, including the right to economic independence (contrasting a Helga who is "established, secure and comfortable" [45] earlier in the text), the right to speak for herself (since, as Michelle Wallace points out, "No one can really speak *for* anyone else"),[21] and, perhaps most importantly, the right to control her own body. The imagined communities in which a feminine birthright can be realized remain all too imagined. Perhaps these "independences" are not ever fully attainable within the contexts in which Helga finds herself, but her descent into the folk represents the greatest limitation on her freedoms. In singling out this discourse, Larsen places it at the low end of the spectrum of possible subject positions.

Loss of control over the body has particular significance because of what the body means in African American literary history. In slavery, the body was not even the property of the embodied, contributing, as Carby points out, to the legitimization of rape and sexual exploitation.[22] Further, Hortense Spillers suggests that given the ways in which slavery and racial oppression have worked on their victims through the category of gender, this "problematizing of gender places [the African American woman] . . . *out* of the traditional symbolics of female gender, and it is our task to make a place for this different social subject."[23] That is, one must consider questions of gender as they regard African American women always with an eye toward questions of race, and realizing this, Larsen gives us the various dilemmas of Helga Crane. For Helga, her body marks not only her racial but also her gender difference; within the intersections of these marks of identity, she searches for a legitimizing, even subversive, discursive space. And it is her difference in terms of gender and sexuality that becomes the primary means by which she searches for a performative identity that she finds suitable and relatively stable. Mary Helen Washington has written that in many novels by African American women, "the fundamental issue is whether or not women can exert control over their sexuality."[24] For Larsen's Helga, the case is no different, for control over her sexuality will ultimately contribute to not only her identity as a woman but also her position within the African American community. The way Helga handles her sexuality — and the ways others interpret it — will determine, to a certain extent, the "authenticity" of her blackness. The discourses of black identity have as some of their basic premises rules for the expression of sexuality that determine one's standing as a racial being.

Cheryl Wall has noted that early on in *Quicksand*, Helga Crane comes to "the incipient realization that sexuality is political; it is 'power.' But Helga mistakenly assumes it is hers to wield."[25] Indeed, Wall astutely observes a relationship between sexuality, politics, and power; I would suggest, however, that "politics" could be more specifically defined as the politics of race: What is one's standing among African Americans, and how does one gain stature and voice within the black community? Further, what sort of power, if any, can Helga salvage from the politics of sexuality? To be sure, Helga's options for expressing her sexuality are limited, but do such limitations necessarily condemn Helga to an inability to act on her own behalf or her own accord? Faced with racism and sexism that mark the boundaries of "acceptable" roles open to her, Helga seeks ways in which she can avoid acquiescing to these limitations. Both Carby and Wall write of "the repression of passion and the repression or denial of female sexuality and desire."[26] But the term "repression" is a loaded one; its connotations are almost exclusively negative, whereas in *Quicksand* such "repression" has at times positive consequences for Helga Crane. Helga's withholding or "repression" of her sexuality is not in every case a failure of character or a construct imposed on her from without; rather, it can represent a control over her body that marks a departure from a tradition that describes the African American female as a creature of "rampant sexuality" unchecked by herself and uncheckable by anyone else.[27] At the same time, this same repression complicates the discourse of black identity by challenging the racist stereotype of the "true" black woman as an oversexed temptress. Repression of sexuality, despite its overtones of psychological pathology, may actually serve as a revisionary tool when applied to certain notions of black identity.

Certainly, I have pointed here to a variety of discourses that have widely different parameters for performance and participation. My intention, however, is to suggest that in performativity, Helga negotiates the various subject positions "offered" to her and, in encountering and sometimes embracing discourses of one kind or another, subverts the primacy and authenticity of any one. If Helga Crane is unhappy with identities thrust on her by virtue of her race, she can control her sexuality in such a way as to change the circumstances and situate herself differently in the discourse of race.

At Naxos, Helga Crane occupies the position of "lady," or more specifically, "Negro lady," with its complex combination of class, race, and gender implications. At the austere school, Helga feels out of place, lost in a world that "was as complicated and rigid in its ramifications as the highest strata of white society" (8). The school resembles E. Franklin Frazier's description of a community of "status without substance."[28] That is, Naxos's ideals are formed only with respect to conformity to highly stylized social convention. Its concern with family background, status, and "connections" equates a "proper" blackness with class position (though obviously one antithetical to the folk), and Helga, attempting to blend into this discourse, relies not only on her education and occupation but also on her engagement to James Vayle. By placing herself in the position of becoming a potential sexual partner and marital possession of Vayle, Helga inserts herself into the discourse of African American elitism. As the narrator notes, this desire for a particular identity "even accounted for her engagement to James" (8). By the end of the first chapter of *Quicksand*, Larsen has related to us the significance of sexuality; because of her marriageability, Helga can potentially assume a position within the discourse of bourgeois authenticity.

The hypocrisy of Naxos and Helga's inability—indeed, unwillingness—to wholeheartedly embrace Afro-Saxon codes of behavior and systems of values drive Larsen's protagonist from the school and from James Vayle. Her final interview with Anderson (who later becomes Anne Grey's husband) before she leaves reinforces the importance of sexuality in Helga's role within this particular African American community. Anderson asks her to stay, proclaiming that she has "dignity and breeding" (21), an innocuous statement on some levels, but one that also points to Helga's perceived potential as a breeder of future generations of Naxos students, teachers, and administrators. "You're a lady," says Anderson, relying specifically on that gendered term for class status, going on to speak of "tendencies inherited from good stock" (21). Helga, weary of references to herself as something like a champion brood sow, reveals the "scandalous" nature of her own conception and flees to Chicago. By invoking miscegenation and illegitimacy, Helga attempts to combine class and sexuality in such a way as to write herself out of Naxos's discourse of elitism.

Giddings suggests that "repulsed by social and cultural limitations intrinsic to the school's philosophy, [Helga] feels that her own 'illegitimate' origins belie her pretensions to the life of an acculturated 'lady.'"[29] Not only do they "belie" her subject position among the Naxos elite, but the invocation of those origins serves as a method of escape from a smothering discourse. Helga performs herself out of Naxos. When not invoking these facts of her past, she fits in well in the eyes of others; even the rigid class distinctions that give Naxos its unique character can be performed by an "illegitimate impostor" such as Helga. Far from suffering from repressed sexuality, Helga flaunts familial sexual history in an effort to regain control over both her own body (in the form of breaking the engagement to Vayle) and the course of her own life.[30]

Escaping from the southern elite to the urban folk, Helga still has to deal with the intersection of race and gender as a determinant of her position within the discourse of black identity. Perhaps she is no longer looked to as the mother of the future elite, but her sexuality is very much an issue. The sexual "horror" of Helga's origins again comes into play when she confronts her uncle's new wife. Mrs. Nilssen admonishes Helga, insisting that "my husband is not your uncle. No indeed! Why, that would make me your aunt!" (29). Mrs. Nilssen's distaste for miscegenation—to which she is connected in the remotest possible way, having known none of the parties involved and sharing none of the "tainted" blood—is so strong that it places a black identity squarely on Helga. Female sexuality, in this case her mother's transgressive sexuality, lends Helga a racial identity, reminding the reader of the bond between discourses of gender, sexuality, and race. Miscegenation by Helga's mother effectively removes her from the discourse of white identity, placing both her—although she is white—and her daughter in a discourse of blackness constructed by whites.

Although Helga cannot conceal the issue of sexuality in the encounter with Mrs. Nilssen (though doing so would only really be important if Helga were seeking to pass, which she is not), Chicago does represent in other ways a new side of her sexuality that must be both acknowledged and controlled. As a visibly black woman on the streets of the urban North, Helga confronts several men who think her a prostitute. Again, Larsen presents us with the stereotype of the African American female as uncontrollably libidinal and even immoral in the practice of her sexuality. Helga chooses to control her sexuality in such a way as to maintain the possibility of an identity that does not compromise her independence, intelligence, and self-definition (i.e., her feminine "birthrights") to a vision of blackness that she finds unacceptable. Larsen's narrator points out that "a few men, both white and black, offered her money, but the price of the money was too dear. Helga Crane did not feel inclined to pay it" (34). Certainly, one could make the case that a white woman in a similar situation could be subject to a parallel categorization; Theodore Dreiser's *Sister Carrie,* for example, represents an analogous, though hardly identical situation (ironically, its setting, too, is Chicago). But Helga's phenotype heightens the probability of such a misinterpretation, and here I find Carby's observation that "the black female [was] excluded . . . from the parameters of virtuous possibilities" particularly influential in shaping my thinking.[31] Helga refuses, however, to let this vision of race deny the possibilities of independence, intellect, and female empowerment that eventually come along in the figure of Mrs. Hayes-Rore.

The introduction of Mrs. Hayes-Rore, "a prominent 'race woman' and authority on the problem" (37), is less a criticism on Larsen's part of the ineffectiveness of the black bourgeoisie's speechifying ("merely patchworks of others' speeches and opinions" [38]) than an insertion into the story of a woman who does in fact control her own destiny. Mrs. Hayes-Rore, widow and activist, represents one possible identity for a self-reliant, educated African American woman. Indeed, Larsen makes clear that the death of Mrs. Hayes-Rore's husband, who "depart[ed] this life hurriedly and unexpectedly and a little mysteriously" (37), makes her own ascent to self-definition possible. Although the wealth and political clout of her late husband facilitate Mrs. Hayes-Rore's movement toward self-definition, it is more this demise of the masculine than the class position she already enjoyed by virtue of marriage that enables her to pursue her various concerns.

Taken from a short sojourn among the Chicago folk, Helga arrives in New York to begin living among the northern urban bourgeoisie. Wall correctly points out that "Helga's Harlemites are possessed of a race consciousness at once consuming and superficial, proud and ineffectual."[32] However, the Harlem chapters of Helga's life are not simply a critique of this segment of black America. In this milieu, Helga not only becomes disentangled from certain male sexual demands (Vayle and the Chicago solicitors) but initially appears to have found an African American identity that corresponds more closely with her own idea of who she is. Helga finally comes "to know people with tastes and ideas similar to her own. Their sophisticated cynical talk, their elaborate parties, the unobtrusive correctness of their clothes and homes, all appealing to her craving for smartness, enjoyment" (43). Helga begins to stake her sense of legitimate identity among the northern urban bourgeoisie without feeling either a pressure toward the highly stratified elitism of Naxos or a necessity to be among the folk.

Eventually, however, Helga grows dissatisfied with her surroundings, both "the crowds of nameless folk on the street" (48) and her New Negro friends who go in for, in Wall's words, the "manufactured blackness" of attempting to adopt and co-opt folk practices, treating them as if they

were goods to be purchased and consumed.³³ It appears that in this epi-
sode of her life, Helga's identity crisis is brought on by a crisis of racial
authenticity. She feels herself to be neither a part of the African American folk nor part of the middle class who write/act themselves into the
folk discourse for political (and fashion) purposes. Helga dismisses Anne's
suggestion that "what's the matter with the Negro race [is that] they
won't stick together" (61) as part of an "inadequate answer" to the question of why a community based on "race" is necessary at all. Implicit here
is the suggestion that intraracial solidarity, which may be reductive of the
subject's multiple simultaneous identity positions, may not hold out the
same promise as a diverse coalition not based on exclusionary or limiting
identity politics. Helga, at this juncture, feels that the only way to surpass
the limitations of such a discourse is "to ignore racial barriers and give
her attention to people" as nonracial people (62). And it is in her decision
to move to Denmark that Helga attempts to subvert such talk of basic
racial division and loyalties. Larsen's detailed attention to the place of race
and sexuality, however, adds another dimension to this predicament, for
it is with the arrival of Naxos's Anderson and the letter and money from
Uncle Peter Nilssen that Helga decides to abandon Harlem in search of
something else.

In what might be one of *Quicksand*'s true scenes of sexual repression,
Helga begins to worry about her renewed relationship with Anderson,
feeling "a strange ill-defined emotion, a vague yearning rising within her"
(50), when the two meet. Helga experiences a sexual attraction for Anderson that she finds both thrilling ("Eagerly she desired to see him again
right away to right herself in his thoughts" [51]) and threatening, given
the nature of their language on her parting Naxos. Helga, now an independent if not entirely happy woman, can see an extended relationship
with Anderson only as a way to fix more permanently her position in
the New Negro society she is growing to despise. Owing to expectations
about her gender, Helga views a possible relationship with Anderson as
quicksand in itself. Tellingly, it is with the word "uplift" (52) that Helga
tries to put Anderson out of her mind and plans. It is the uplift philosophy of Naxos that wanted her as a breeder of "good stock" (21). To the
uplift mentality, Helga imputes the need continually to discuss and assert
racial identity in a programmatic fashion; she wonders "with unreasoning
exasperation, why [those in Anderson's circle] didn't . . . find something

else to talk about" (52).[34] For a character such as Helga, who has already written herself into and out of discourses of blackness on several levels, each time sacrificing some other part of her identity, tying her fortunes to Anderson could only trap her in an unsatisfactory subject position.

As this turmoil over gender roles and sexuality grows, the letter from Peter Nilssen arrives. Essentially, it amounts to a payoff to keep the sexual misdeeds of Helga's mother forever hidden. Ironically, by buying Helga's silence—"you understood thoroughly that I must terminate my outward relation with you" (54)—Nilssen enables Helga to escape Harlem, Anderson, and New Negro society in an effort to prove her assertion that her growing distaste for Harlem "wasn't merely a matter of color. It was something broader, deeper, that made folk kin" (55). At the same time, it gives Helga a financial position she had been unable to achieve even as an independent, working woman; "And now she was free," the narrator proclaims (58), suggesting the enormous import of the five thousand dollars. And so Helga sails for Denmark in search of an identity that is not determined by notions of "race" that carry the baggage of our unique American racialist hegemony. In shifting cultures, Helga sees the opportunity to revise her performance of "race." She heads for the European continent, the heart of Western culture virtually "untainted" by blackness of any sort, to determine if she can arrive at an identity that feels complete and unhampered by conflicting expectations of racial and gender roles.

Much has been made of the Denmark section of *Quicksand,* and with good reason, since through it Larsen demonstrates even further the complexities and interrelation between race and gender. Hailed and presented to Danish society as an exotic, Helga comes to a new understanding of her complex identity as an African American woman when she rejects painter Axel Olsen's sexual advances and marriage proposal. McDowell interprets this climactic scene as Helga's "awareness of her legacy of rape and concubinage at the hands of white men, a legacy which compels her to decline Olsen's sexual proposition and his marriage proposal."[35] Wall writes that "this scene more than any other shows how inextricably bound sexual and racial identity are."[36] And both critics are absolutely correct; it is not merely blackness that makes Helga an exotic, but rather her gender and others' sexual desire in combination with her race. Her experience in Denmark recalls the comment of Toomer's narrator in "Bona and Paul," who remarks on Bona's relationship to Paul that African American "men like him (Paul) can fascinate. One is not responsible for fascination."[37] Within this system of erotic exchange, blackness inscribes exoticism on the body; the discourse of desire is a significant part of the discourse of "race." The Danes consider Helga "attractive, unusual, in an exotic, almost savage sort of way" (70), and her aunt and uncle dress her in "barbaric bracelets . . . dangling ear-rings . . . [and] beads about her neck" (70), not to mention a "leopard-skin coat . . . [and] turban-like hats" (74), in both parody and approximation of the allure of the "Dark Continent." Of course, Helga is about as familiar with Africa as the Danes themselves. The portrait of Helga that Olsen paints (which he considers "the true Helga Crane" [88]), seems to Helga not "herself at all, but some disgusting sensual creature with her features" (89). In taking leave of the African American "race obsession" with which she found fault in New Negro society, Helga ends up re-placing herself into a discourse in which her identity is still inscribed in racial terms that are no less loaded with assumptions about gender and sexuality. The parameters of performance for notions of black authenticity are altered, but they do not vanish.

In fact, Helga finds herself in a position with a striking similarity to her condition in Chicago. Before proposing marriage, Olsen asks Helga to become his mistress, and Helga rejects him on both accounts. Part of her reply to his advances is illuminating; she states, "I'm not for sale. Not to you. Not to any white man. I don't at all care to be owned" (87). Helga herself brings race to this discussion of sexuality. She casts Olsen's offer in terms of the African American woman as possessable commodity, re-emphasizing the position of femininity within certain discourses of race. Although it appears in the text that on some level, Helga always desired an identity that conformed in some respects to that of the white bourgeoisie, Larsen dispels the desirability of that position in demystifying the importance of race, gender, and sexuality within this "master" narrative itself. And again we see that to break from the stereotype of the black woman, Helga must exercise control over her sexuality. By refusing to give her body to Olsen, she extricates herself from the discourse into which he has literally painted her. The consequence, however, is that Helga Crane is left again without a satisfactory identity that can accommodate both her gender and race birthrights.

Larsen takes the further step of illuminating the performative aspects of identity by providing insight into why Helga's "old unhappy questioning mood came upon her again, insidiously stealing away more of the contentment from her transformed existence" (83). The narrator reports that on visiting a minstrel show in Copenhagen, Helga "was shocked at the avidity at [*sic*] which Olsen beside her drank it in" (83). Initially this is a critique of white middle-class fetishizing of blackness as both the exotic and the absurd, but it is Helga who "returned again and again to the Circus," seeing in the minstrel show her "fused doubts, rebellion, expediency, and urgent longings" (83). On the one hand, her continued pilgrimage to minstrelsy is a self-conscious recognition of the role she performs within Danish society; going to the Circus is akin to looking in the (Danish) mirror. On the other hand, this spectacle of performed blackness fuels Helga's desire to adopt yet another style of performance. It contributes to her recurrence of "race consciousness," with which she rebukes Olsen and his politics of race and sexuality; she tells him, "I couldn't marry a white man. . . . it's racial" (88), after having seen the way in which he is willing to accept the exaggerations and distortions of the minstrel show as a paradigm of blackness. These same excesses aid Helga, who has a better sense of what types of performance are more or less "authentic" with respect to African American identity, come to the conclusion that she is "homesick . . . for Negroes" (92), the very African Americans she has spent much of the book despising. Her performed identity in white bourgeois society remains too interconnected with a sense of irreducible racial difference — though the Danes "rated it a precious thing" (83) — for Helga, who has spent the entire novel searching for a community with flexible standards of cultural identity, to accept.

As a result, Helga returns to New York seeking to reconnect with "these mysterious, these terrible, these fascinating, these lovable, dark hordes. Ties that were of the spirit. Ties that not only superficially entangled with mere outline of features or color of skin. Deeper. Much deeper than either of these" (95). It becomes apparent that Helga will seek her niche within the discourse of black identity on the basis of "race." Yet the language of the passage casts doubt on the viability of such a connection. Helga generalizes African Americans as alien, curious others, re-presenting in some fashion the type of "blackness as otherness" she experiences in Europe; this time, however, she decides to embrace that categorization. Although the narrator denies it is primarily darkness that lends one both status and community, we can see from the last quotation that the "ties of the spirit" that give this sense of community and identity remain nebulous at best. Helga seeks a discourse of black identity not based on skin color alone but grounded in a cultural and spiritual similarity. She redefines herself in terms of a discourse of "race" that is less easily dissected and categorized than those she has previously experienced. Her attempts at self-defined race and gender roles, thwarted by repeated confrontations with constructions of "naturalized" and immutable difference, lead her to a solidarity and shared identity based on an otherness from "mainstream" American culture—but a difference, it appears, that is not easily named. Helga retreats to the relative safety of identity as "knowable" only through the bond of "natural race," rather than risking isolation through a continued insistence on the performance of more concrete factors that may characterize particular notions of racial identity. In addition, this new resolution to find identity in a "spiritual" black community involves a change in the way Helga expresses her sexuality.

This process of reidentification through which Helga proceeds—which is eventually responsible for her death—strongly echoes Butler's description of the dangers of certain forms of identity politics. The almost hopeless determinism at the end of *Quicksand* finds an analogue in theory when Butler writes:

> The despair evident in some forms of identity politics is marked by the elevation and regulation of identity-positions *as* a primary political policy. When the articulation of coherent identity becomes its own policy, the policing of identity takes the place of a politics in which identity works dynamically in the service of a broader cultural struggle toward the rearticulation and empowerment of groups that seeks [*sic*] to overcome the dynamic of repudiation and exclusion by which "coherent subjects" are constituted.[38]

In ultimately rendering herself more "knowable" through certain standards of performance, Helga finds herself more firmly mired in the quicksand of competing gender and racial roles. Although she believes her return to New York will offer a liberating space, she comes to find her political options more limited and her identity positions further regulated.

No longer avoiding performing herself into a community that requires a choice between racial solidarity and nonexploitative gender roles, Helga returns to Harlem as a sexual being. Not content to be an object from which pleasure can be derived, Helga moves to affirm and validate her own sexual desires. That is, she adopts a new set of performative guidelines that open a discursive space that acknowledges her sexuality as an integral and positive part of her identity. She remakes her appearance, fetishized in Europe, into a "deliberate lure" to attract and to "expect . . . admiration as her due" (98). At a party where she encounters ex-fiancé James Vayle, she spurns his idea that the value of her sexuality lies in having children to help the race "get somewhere," saying, "I for one don't intend to contribute any to the cause" (103). The "new" Helga seeks a discourse in which she can value sexuality in its own right, further evidence of which can be found in her efforts to cultivate a friendship with Audrey Denney, the woman whose sexuality—she dances with white men, which "can only mean one thing" (61)—infuriates Anne Grey's New Negro, and rather prudish, sensibility. Within these new parameters of performance, Helga attempts to fabricate a new identity at the convergence of positive aspects of womanhood, race, and sexuality.

Hostetler asserts, however, that "coming home to Harlem ends tragically for Helga because she is unable to reconcile her sexual awakening with her developing sense of identity as a black woman."[39] Again, an existing discourse of identity—one in which race and gender collide—comes into conflict with Helga's revisionist performance, the terms of her "new" performance becoming subsumed within those of the more established discourse. Helga imagines herself the lover of Anderson, now Anne's husband, and plays into the tradition of concubinage that she has resisted in previous scenes of *Quicksand*. In making this choice of a sexual partner, Helga somewhat unwittingly reinserts herself into a discourse that inscribes her sexuality with immorality, libidinous nature, and temptation. Although she seeks to disrupt such a discourse with negative connotations for black female sexuality in favor of one of self-actualization, Helga's performance is rather easily reinterpreted into negative terms of black womanhood. After Anderson apologizes for his advances, Helga accidentally, yet fittingly for Larsen's sense of irony, finds her way into the African American folk. Anderson's "rejection" of her places Helga, in some way, outside the bourgeois society she grudgingly admires. The narrator relates that "Helga Crane wasn't, after all, a rebel from society, from Negro society. . . . She had no wish to stand alone. But these late fears [that her "affair" might be exposed] were overwhelmed by the hardiness of insistent desire" (107). Insistent desire (the recognition of, and urge to, satisfy natural sexual impulses), implies the narrator, disqualifies Helga from the black bourgeoisie, forcing her to turn elsewhere in search of a discursive space in which to reconcile her birthrights. Her conversion (which is ostensibly religious but also has deep significance for her continuing development of both race and gender identity), the scene that immediately follows these thoughts, marks a shift in her identity from northern urban bourgeoisie to southern rural folk.

Larsen's language during the scene of Helga's conversion points to the ways in which the birthrights of womanhood and blackness are, in fact, irreconcilable in *Quicksand*. Larsen satirizes the "saving grace" of folk identity and community by making the church and its congregation emblematic of the quicksand of gender and race in which Helga will eventually drown. Helga, looking most nonbourgeois on her entrance into the storefront church, finds herself, at first reaction, ludicrously out of place: "She sat down on the floor, a dripping heap, and laughed and laughed and laughed" (111). Her response, though inappropriate for such a solemn religious ceremony, leads the congregation to draw conclusions about her person. The ornately dressed though extremely disheveled Helga, who laughs at their folk religion (a reaction due, in part, to her class bias), becomes "a scarlet 'oman" (112) and "errin' sistah" intent on mocking their morality. The congregation, however, continues singing its hymn with patriarchal verses such as "Yet He found me, I beheld Him, / Bleeding on the cursed tree; / Heard Him pray: 'Forgive them, Father,'" ending in the refrain "Less of self and more of Thee" (111–12). To this Larsen adds:

> Behind Helga somewhere a *woman* had begun to cry audibly, and soon, somewhere else, another. . . . Helga too began to weep, at first silently and softly; then with great racking sobs. Her nerves were so torn, so aching, her body so wet so cold! It was a relief to cry unrestrainedly. (112, my emphasis)

The scene presents the nexus of Helga's identity troubles.[40] It brings together questions of race, gender, class, and geography as they pertain to Helga's search for a discourse of black identity suitable to her own experience. The unnamed woman's display of emotion, presumably a result of intense spirituality, contrasts nicely with Helga's emotional reaction toward the "failure" of her latest attempt at performing a viable alternative identity. The woman in the church desires to bring herself further into a discourse, while Helga's discourse has just been shattered. Note, too, that Helga's crying (indeed, her presence at the meeting at all), brought on by her rejection by a man, proves to be a relief for her own body. Helga continues to be body centered, hoping to realize her own identity by controlling her physical being, while ostensibly the church wants her intangible soul.

Larsen, however, subverts this body-spirit description. The narrator proclaims that "Helga Crane was amused, angry, disdainful, as she sat there, listening to the preacher praying for her soul" (113). But eventually the service becomes more than merely spiritual, taking on "an almost Bacchic vehemence," becoming a "weird orgy"(113). With those small phrases, Larsen links body and soul; spiritual salvation and physical revels become one. By extension, Helga must yield both in body and in spirit to achieve an identity among the (religious) folk.

The congregation offers her a chance to "come to Jesus," to join their community, adopt their patterns of belief and behavior, and find a place "unburdened by the complexities of life as she had known it" (114). The solution represented here by the African American folk and their religious tradition is not for a woman to gain control over her own body but, ironically, for her to submit herself to a patriarchal god. Woman must relinquish herself to masculine authority, Larsen implies, if she is to have a place in this community. Larsen specifically mentions the reactions of women to the service: "The writhings and weeping of the feminine portion . . . seemed to predominate" (113), and they "crawled over the floor like reptiles" (114) in giving thanks for Helga's salvation. Women are the ones most visibly and audibly giving themselves to the Lord, though in their submission they are implicitly subhuman.

Helga decides to join this community. Hostetler holds that "in Larsen's view, to succumb to a preexisting paradigm means to accept one pattern, one stereotype, at the expense of growth or change, cutting oneself off from identity as process and dialogue."[41] In going south to the rural folk with Pleasant Green, Helga abandons her attempt to reformulate hierarchies of womanhood and blackness through the performance of various identities. She submits to "the mysterious grandeur and holiness of far-off simpler centuries" (114) by placing herself within a patriarchal social system that severely limits her range of possible identities. Her "seduction" of

Green creates for her a "new status as a preacher's wife" (118); she receives an opportunity to enter into an African American community, but only at the expense of subordinating herself to the masculine. Helga's identity is dependent on "that rattish yellow man" (117) who is her husband.

As I mentioned earlier, Helga initially attempts to assert her identity in terms of "uplift" behaviors, but she fails. Through this she learns not only that class differences implicit in such a notion interfere with a "connection" to the folk but also that it takes more than an individually felt sense of connection to become part of a community. Helga has to be "broken" of her bourgeois attitudes before her performance among the folk becomes fully accepted. When she reaches the point in her life where she has "no time for the pursuit of beauty, or for the uplifting of other harassed teeming women, or for the instruction of their neglected children" (124), Helga is on her way to a more fully folk identity. It is only when she practices an "utter yielding to what had been sent her . . . [that] her husband's flock began to approve and commend this submission and humility to a superior wisdom" (126). When Helga accepts that it is "natu'al fo' a 'oman to hab chilluns" (125) and that "in de nex' worl' we's all recompense'" for the constant and thankless toil of this one, she is performing like a female member of the folk. In those parameters, she finds community.

Of course, the conclusion of *Quicksand*—as so many critics have pointed out—does not validate the desirability of female folk identity. Eventually Helga rejects these folk practices and this community as an acceptable alternative to her past experiences. She refuses the religion that facilitated her entrance into the folk, recognizing that "for Negroes at least," particularly the community in which she finds herself, life is "only a great disappointment," not a blessing from a God "she knew . . . didn't exist" (130). Although confined to her sickbed, Helga attempts to destabilize her position within this religious community by having blasphemous stories read to her. Helga considers leaving the community as a way "to escape from the oppression, the degradation, that her life had become" (135). It is through her body now, however, that she has become tied to the community. Helga balks at leaving her children, and thus the range of her possible performances is greatly reduced. It becomes "hard to think out a feasible way of retrieving all those agreeable, desired things" (135) of her prefolk existence and support a family simultaneously. In contrast to the more ideological impediments to her performances earlier in the novel,

Helga now finds herself bound by sheer physical limits such as providing food for her children and her own failing health. Ironically, as Helga struggles throughout *Quicksand* to enact and subvert ideas about her own body—the authenticity of "race" and the "proper" place of gender and sexuality—she becomes locked in a discourse that asserts its power in and through her body itself. Her ever-narrowing spectrum of alternatives closes out. The choice of life or death supersedes the choice of *how* to live. Her only escape from this identity lies not in performance but in death.

The discourse that privileges this type of folk existence is involved necessarily in restricting the discourse of female identity. Like Janie's marriage to Logan Killicks in Zora Neale Hurston's *Their Eyes Were Watching God*, Helga Crane's relationship with Green involves accepting a subordinate role because of gender. Unlike Janie, however, Helga's body becomes inscribed in such a way as to preclude all alternatives but one. In this folk community connected by race, class, and geography, female biology proves the community's most indelible marker. Helga can perform herself in, but she can never leave. Once the feminine is subordinated according to social convention, nature works to keep it subordinated. The African American woman might "go on de muck" to develop a relationship with the folk, but she also risks drowning in that same muck. For Larsen, geography, class, race, and gender are inextricably linked factors in creating identity; the tragedy is that the female has to be submerged or relegated to a second-class position to create an identity that finds acceptance in a wide range of communities. If Hughes's "Cross" delineates the discourse of black identity by asking where someone "neither black nor white" dies, Larsen's *Quicksand* complicates it by showing why black women die in that poem's shacks. They have the potential to wind up in a fine, big house, independent and self-sufficient, but they achieve that goal only at the risk of alienating themselves from communities both black and white.

# 5

## Color, Culture, and the Nature of Race: George S. Schuyler's *Black No More*

Although 1931, the year of publication for George S. Schuyler's *Black No More: Being an Account of the Strange and Wonderful Workings of Science in the Land of the Free, A.D. 1933–1940,* is after what many scholars date the end of the Harlem Renaissance, Henry Louis Gates Jr. claims that this work is a "famous satirical novel about the self-consciousness of the Harlem Renaissance . . . that many of us still teach today."[1] Because of this self-consciousness, Schuyler's book seems a particularly apt text to examine at this stage. Schuyler not only sets forth competing claims of racial identity but also asks his readers to examine relationships between identity, community, culture, and politics. Schuyler, like Larsen, Toomer, and Johnson, is interested in the ways in which racial identity may be constructed, deconstructed, and reconstructed in literature, particularly in terms of settings, characters, and their circumstances within a fictional world. It is via a self-conscious assessment of malleable, potentially unsteady markers of identity that Schuyler begins to reshape the ends to which concepts of identity might most productively be employed. Through developing notions of racial performance, he questions the adequacy of "race"as a descriptive term, and in devaluing certain descriptive powers of "race," he refocuses attention on the value "race" has as a tool for maintaining political, social, and aesthetic hierarchies. In restructuring these hierarchies, Schuyler suggests some interesting possibilities for a retheorization of both literary and political practices that revolve around notions of difference and a cultural geography of center and margin.

Gates writes that "Schuyler's position in the black intellectual community was one of critic from within. Schuyler constructed his intellectual role as that of a dissident, reserving his animus for his fellow black intellectuals, and cultivating critical skepticism as his calling."[2] In launching a critique of blackness from within the African American intellectual community, Schuyler also reappraises whiteness as a benchmark by which to judge identity and culture. In creating a novel in which almost all the black characters are actually "white" and all the white characters "black," Schuyler is able to examine the question of "birthright" that Johnson and others raise by modifying the theme of passing in such a way as to render it an issue of culture rather than color. By creating this world in which all people are both/neither black and/nor white, Schuyler moves toward a theory of "race" that turns on radical reevaluations of the locus of difference and the value of that difference in the construction of community. And in embracing science fiction as a genre, he avoids a telescoping of romanticism, nature, and racial innocence/savagery; in making machine culture squarely the center of his narrative, Schuyler prevents the equation of "racial" essence with pretechnological times, asking his readers to consider the ways in which "race" itself is as much a significant cultural tool as the cotton gin or Model A.

Certainly, all the issues I have just mentioned require more detailed explanation than I have given them here, and I shall return to them more fully later in this chapter. I mention them now, however, because they indicate that Schuyler's ultimate goal in *Black No More* is to denaturalize race. By emphasizing class, gender, and geography, Schuyler sets forth to demonstrate the learned pattern of "racial" being and the ways in which "race" is a highly unstable category, although it simultaneously serves as a usable central trope in terms of establishing social order in the United States. Eventually, *Black No More* stands as a challenge to the hegemony of race that Schuyler sees both blacks and whites of every political persuasion embracing. In coming to understand Schuyler's critique, I shall investigate several aspects of Schuyler's literary imagination and philosophy of race. First, I will explore the ways in which he configures color as culture; second comes an evaluation of Schuyler's assertions of color and culture as completely separate entities; third is an investigation of both "race" and community as performed, codified, and learned social roles; and finally I shall delve into the connections Schuyler makes between performance, hegemony, "race consciousness," and the discontents of writing "race." That is, if Johnson's narrator in *The Autobiography of an Ex-Colored Man* achieves some sort of race consciousness by the end of the novel, what are the consequences for Schuyler's unrepentant, unremorseful ex-coloreds at the conclusion of *Black No More*? Schuyler is more complex than labels such as "assimilationist," "conservative," and "iconoclast" can make him out to be. While he was, more or less, all those things, it was Schuyler's mission in *Black No More* to demonstrate that such labeling leads precisely to continued inequality and division in the United States.

## Color as Culture

If George Schuyler is a constructionist in terms of "race" and racial difference, he is also a product of the culture in which he lived. His constructionism was a reaction, at least in part, to an essentialist view of race he came across every day; and, indeed, his approach to, and vision of, "race" categories in *Black No More* and many of his other writings has been the source of much critical controversy. It is my purpose in this section, however, to read several passages from *Black No More* in which Schuyler appears to abandon a constructivist attitude toward "race" for a more essentialist position and, in doing so, draw some conclusions about the extent to which Schuyler was influenced by—and part of—a racialist hegemony that naturalized cultural differences between black and white as biological, innate, or organic.

The term "Black Culture" was, and still is, a phrase with significant resonances for "race" and its ability to define certain practices and delineate difference. What stands among the central concerns of *Black No More* is the ends to which this type of differentiation is employed. Although certain cultural practices may productively be discussed as originating in various racial communities, what are the consequences of setting up such distinctions as markers of "authentic" identity? Gino Speranza, writing in 1925, states that "after fifty years of freedom, [the Negro race] has been unavoidably segregated both physically and culturally."[3] Speranza calls this case "tragic" because it appears to him that African Americans are unassimilable, representing a roadblock to "complete American conformity."[4] Blackness and the cultural practices developing from slavery, segregation, and oppression pose difficulties for an America he imagines as primarily white, Anglo-Saxon, and Protestant. I present Speranza's view to help illustrate one way in which color helps to define culture. Black and white mark separate terrains. The challenge of *Black No More* is to acknowledge this difference while working to undermine it on a philosophical level. Schuyler attempts to reinvent both African American and American cultural traditions so that these types of distinctions between them diminish or disappear.

Schuyler recognized that one can, indeed, discuss the separateness of black and white in a Jim Crow society, though in doing so, one risks a racial essentialization that is contrary to his own philosophy of "race." Looking back on travels he made in the 1920s from the perspective of an avowed conservative in 1966, Schuyler writes that he

> came to detect the varying nuances [in race relations that] make communities distinctive, and these influences on the direction of Negro life. To me the myth of white "hatred" of Negroes was soon dissipated. I learned it was dangerous to generalize . . . [and that] people were humans and individuals before they were racial stereotypes.[5]

While the passage reads, in some respects, like a platitudinous television spot from the AD Council against racism ("People are people; don't be prejudiced"), it does point to an apparent contradiction in Schuyler's thinking. People are all humans and individuals, yet there remains such a thing as a collective, racialized "Negro life." Is this a flaw in Schuyler's philosophy? Is he trying to establish a "basic" African American subject position while maintaining a belief in irreducible human heterogeneity as well as a sense of homogeneous "humanity" that supersedes categories of "race"? Even from the perspective of his own carefully crafted autobiography, Schuyler appears unable or unwilling to determine how to use constructs of "black" and "white" in a strategy that moves toward redefining both.

If we turn our attention to *Black No More,* however, we perhaps gain a perspective on how and why this ambiguity about color as culture comes about. Near the beginning of the novel, Schuyler—through a narrator privileged, in this moment, to protagonist Max/Matt's consciousness[6]—sets up a curious distinction between black and white cultures:

> There was something lacking in these ofay places of amusement or else there was something present that one didn't find in the black-and-tan resorts in Harlem. The joy and abandon here was obviously forced. . . . The Negroes, it seemed to him, were much gayer, enjoyed themselves more deeply [than whites] and yet they were more restrained, actually more refined.[7]

African Americans are happy and spontaneous, traits attributed to blackness in the American racialist discourse, yet the narrator begins to undermine those images by calling them "more refined." At the same time, Schuyler indulges even more racial stereotypes about African Americans having "rhythm," with the narrator describing white dancers who are "lumbering couples, out of step half the time and working as strenuously as stevedores emptying the bowels of a freighter . . . noisy, awkward, inelegant" (40). Significantly, he portrays these "black" characteristics as superior to their "white" counterparts; "race" becomes a category on which we can base qualitative distinctions between groups and individuals. Certainly, in a novel considered a satire, we need to look at some of this description with a skeptical eye, yet here is one of the first delineations of the difference "race" makes. Max/Matt (who at this stage is already "white," having undergone Crookman's process of racial transfiguration) waxes nostalgic for "his people," and although Harry Williams tells us that Schuyler was raised to believe that "the term [Negro] was merely a descriptive one and did not mean a specific race" in terms of basic cultural difference, I suggest that here is a problematic moment in the text, an instance in which Schuyler moves beyond irony to link color and cultural performance.[8] Although this description is filtered through the point of view of Max/Matt's consciousness, the authorial decision to present to the readers these musings points to their import. If they are more than just narrative filler, Max/Matt's thoughts suggest the possibility of (or at least the strong presence of the belief in) "race" as a fundamental, distinguishing characteristic in American life. Recalling the lament of Johnson's ex-colored man over his "birthright," the text invites us to take Max/Matt's remorse at leaving his race seriously.

Max/Matt, in shedding his dark skin color, seems lost in a culture not his own. So race does indeed make a difference; color is culture, as Schuyler reinforces later in the novel when he suggests that with the whitening process at its height, "gone was the almost European atmosphere of every Negro ghetto" around the country (87). In stressing European, Schuyler points to cultural difference. Blackness—like Europe—is alien or foreign to a prevailing sense of American culture; it marks a measurable departure from the dominant white American society. The question remains, however, as to why Schuyler chooses to create these passages in which "race" and culture are naturalized into a single package. For a person for whom color is supposedly no more than a descriptor of physical appearance, what ends can be achieved by making color more than phenotype?

The answer lies, at least in part, in Schuyler's understanding of racialist hegemony in the United States. Using Max/Matt's initially essentialist reactions as a foil to constructivist alternatives, Schuyler opens up a space for discussions of slippages, inconsistencies, and ambivalences that continually invade notions of racial essence and construction. If we investigate the disjunctions between character and author, we may be able to see how Schuyler begins to establish a matrix in which multiple discourses of "race" can be played out at the same time. Far from providing a level playing field, however, Schuyler, in putting forth these essentialist positions, gives himself something to knock down; he creates a straw man partially within the protagonist himself, because Max/Matt has been trained to conceive of "race" in the essentialist ways. Schuyler, like Max/Matt in later portions of *Black No More,* recognizes that "people have been raised on the Negro problem, they're used to it, they're trained to react to it" (137), and he subverts the obstacle of essential racial difference by embracing it. At the same time that he posits "race" as a factor that binds together communities, he works in other ways to tear "race" down as a barrier to a larger sense of community.

As Max/Matt contemplates moving into the world as a "white" man, he reflects that in his relationship with his best friend, Bunny, "there would be a wider gulf separating them: the great sea of color" (43). While acknowledging a DuBoisian double consciousness, a twoness of being

American and black, Schuyler also seeks to reconcile that split by dismantling "race" as a term that establishes social order. Schuyler turns revolutionary by draining the great sea of color of all its dangerous and supposedly uncrossable waters. Although Max/Matt, still in the initial stages of culture shock brought on by his racial conversion, voices his displeasure at the "hard, materialistic, grasping, inbred society of whites" (63), Schuyler erases the racial aspect of this characterization by having Max/Matt (with the aid of Bunny) become not only a successful capitalist and fund-raiser for the Knights of Nordica (Schuyler's parody of the Ku Klux Klan) but also an embezzler who leaves no more "than a thousand bucks in the treasury" (194) of the Knights of Nordica by the end of the novel. Max/Matt, who is continuously aware of his "roots" throughout *Black No More,* is as grasping, manipulative, and hard as any character in the book, the white supremacist Snobbcraft included. Apparently, the chase for the materialist American Dream need not be hindered by genetic background.

Williams has asserted that in his youth, Schuyler learned that "the avenue for escape from the Negro caste system was Anglo-bourgeois assimilative behavior."[9] Certainly, Schuyler wants to escape the caste system (and perhaps Max/Matt's transformation is even a symbol of assimilative behavior, in terms of assimilating into a capitalist system), but in this move, Schuyler attempts to break the bond between "Anglo" and "bourgeois," dismantling conceptions of color as culture (or, in this case, color as class). Not only does Schuyler in *Black No More* take a stance contradicting this type of conflation of race and the possibilities of cultural status, but he does so in other writings as well, declaring disgust at those who show surprise that "within the Negro group are social circles quite as cultured and refined as those existing among whites."[10] While recognizing the development of separate cultures on the basis of "race," *Black No More* works to undermine the "naturalness" of such social order. Jim Crow not only functions as a system of physical separation but attempts to fix cultural status as well. Separate can never be equal because that separation is based on the assumption of inequality to begin with. Pointing to the existence of an intellectual equality (as well as a shared capacity for avarice) between races, Schuyler attempts to defamiliarize his reader with the culture-color link by questioning the connections made between phenotype and behavior.

Not only the effects but also the origins of the "color as culture" phenomenon interest the author of *Black No More*. I have already touched on Schuyler's sensitivity to a white hegemony that maintains the discursive model of racial "natures" as a method of maintaining social order. For Schuyler, however, the tragedy is not only the type of oppressive system imposed from without but also an acceptance of that system from within via internalized racism. Schuyler makes plain the effect that internalized racism has on the characters in his novel. Of African Americans in general, he writes, "A lifetime of being Negroes in the United States had convinced them that there was a great advantage in being white" (57). Of Max/Matt: "As a boy he had been taught to look up to white folks as just a little less than gods" (63). Of Shakespeare Agamemnon Beard, the novel's parody of W. E. B. DuBois, Schuyler states: "The learned doctor wrote scholarly and biting editorials in *The Dilemma* denouncing the Caucasians whom he secretly admired and lauding the greatness of the Negroes whom he alternately pitied and despised" (90). And of Dr. Crookman's motives for creating the Black-No-More process: "He was so interested in the continued progress of the American Negroes that he wanted to remove all obstacles in their path by depriving them of their racial characteristics" (55).

Significantly, Schuyler centers his critiques on the phenotypical aspects of race; blackness is despised because it is black, whiteness admired for whiteness' sake. Crookman and Beard, as "learned men," stand as examples that color need not necessarily equal a difference in (intellectual) achievement or the capacity to generate either technology or ideas. Both characters, however, though they should "know better," develop a self-hatred based not on cultural inferiority (their education is no different from, and perhaps even superior to, that of much of the white elite) but rather on hegemonically imposed notions of racial difference. Although they recognize the false premise of "color as culture," they have so internalized the notion that they set about reproducing it in the name of liberation. Beard emphasizes color as culture through his championing of the African American folk, whose distinct status he maintains by writing of "the sufferings and privations of the downtrodden black workers with whose lives he was totally and thankfully unfamiliar" (90). What we see here is an example of the danger of replacing the terms "race" or "ethnicity" with the superficially kinder and gentler "culture." Beyond having resonances for Schuyler's work, I would suggest that this type of linguistic substitution also has repercussions for the contemporary practice of "cultural studies." We must remain vigilant not to renaturalize the term "culture" (which, by definition, must always be a complex social construct)—not to allow it to slip back into the same simplistic, inaccurate, and pernicious power to categorize, essentialize, and reify social relations that the term "race" had in the past.

Of course, part of the critique of Beard is the exaggerated, broad derision of satire, yet what seems of greater political import is the way in which Schuyler apparently impugns Beard's (DuBois's) sincerity and interest in the "folk." Although I think one might be hard-pressed to prove DuBois's work dealing with the folk disingenuous, what is of more importance to Schuyler's satire is the *relationship* between Beard and the folk. The satire is directed not so much at the validity of the subject Beard chooses but at the fact that he is already working from a position of relative inequality with the folk. He makes his connection with the "masses" by writing himself into a discourse of identity that he can also write himself out of with relative ease. And whereas Beard would certainly experience the same racism as the folk on many levels, Schuyler wants to make clear that Beard has other, perhaps less oppressive, discourses of identity available to him simultaneously. Beard, Schuyler suggests, takes advantage of existing intraracial difference to put forth, and get noticed, some concept of the unity of black culture. In the end, Schuyler is offering a critique of Talented Tenth and black bourgeoisie notions of "race consciousness" more so than a personal attack on DuBois himself. Crookman, in a much more obvious manner, proves the power of the talisman of "color as culture" simply by believing he can eradicate cultural difference and inequality ("continued progress") simply by obliterating color.[11]

For Schuyler as a constructionist, however, neither of these methods proves ultimately to be an acceptable alternative, for both work at reproducing and strengthening hegemony although they superficially appear as liberating struggles against it.[12] In rejecting color as culture, Schuyler saw an alternative in creating a vision of American culture as common to all, regardless of race, and dismantling the color-culture hegemonic discourse by infiltrating and subverting the hegemonic power structure itself. In fact, Schuyler will not adopt, like Speranza, a notion of American culture as all white. As American culture exists within the world of *Black No More,* it is fundamentally racist/racialist, and this is unacceptable. What

Schuyler attempts to do, however, is reimagine and reinvent America and its culture in such a way that contributions by people of various "races" are not necessarily "racial" contributions. In *Black No More,* this vision finds a cognate in Max/Matt's directorship and sabotage of the Knights of Nordica; he uses the racist/racialist power structure already in place to dismantle itself. And such a move is possible only because Max/Matt, as a black/white man, understands precisely the intricacies of a racist cultural apparatus. Further, that possibility indicates that "white" culture is not the exclusive "property" of white people; rather, it is shared and understood across racial lines because it affects, is supported by, and is struggled against by people of all races. Indeed, it is a common culture because it holds everyone within its compass. It may be imposed on African Americans from without (that is, for example, laws may be created without the presence of African American's in the legislature), but that does not mean there is no African American participation in "white culture," nor does it imply that African Americans cannot help to shape its direction via experiences that are "race" specific.

Such a refutation of color as culture recalls one of Schuyler's best-known theoretical works, as well as the more famous response to it by Langston Hughes. Schuyler sets about asserting that "artistic performance by colored American artists would in the very nature of things be indistinguishable from other American art."[13] In his piece "The Negro-Art Hokum," Schuyler promotes the idea of colorless American culture; that is, he denies the possibility of art having a distinguishing, authentic character based on race alone. He writes that "Negro art there has been, is, and will be among the numerous black nations of Africa; but to suggest the possibility of any such development among the ten million colored people of this republic is self-evident foolishness."[14] He goes on from this proposition to suggest that even African American folk art is not necessarily "black" art, stating that the folk arts are

> contributions of a caste in a certain section of the country. They are foreign to Northern Negroes, West Indian Negroes, and African Negroes. They are no more expressive or characteristic of the Negro race than the music and dancing of the Appalachian highlanders or the Dalmatian peasantry are expressive or characteristic of the Caucasian race.[15]

Schuyler's insistence on class and geography as the truly formative influences of "racial" culture not only shows him as a racial constructionist but also exhibits his conscious decision not to write himself into a racial ideology that he feels is alien to his own experience. In his attack on "black" art is the suggestion that there exist multiple simultaneous authentic subject positions available for African Americans, positions deeply influenced by such apparently "nonracial" factors as geography and nationality. He further explodes "color as culture" connections by deeming the linkage not revolutionary but reactionary, claiming that it "is probably the last stand of the old myth palmed off by Negrophobists . . . that there are 'fundamental, eternal, and inescapable differences' between white and black Americans."[16] Implicit here also, however, is a critique of the "race pride" school of thought. Looking for fundamental racial difference in the name of establishing racial unity as the basis for political action proves problematic as well. Liberation, Schuyler believes, cannot be achieved simply by reproducing—under the guise of race consciousness—a theory of difference that has its origins in subjugation and oppression. He favors the exploitation of contradictions in racist/racialist thought to make such philosophy collapse on itself over a frontal assault drawn along lines of difference. His position, however, assumes that discriminatory institutions are penetrable by "others," that somehow these institutions will begin to admit difference to their ranks without being forced or pressured from outside, perhaps even by the sort of "race-conscious" discourse that he eschews. Schuyler discounts the value, perhaps even the necessity, of opposition based along lines of difference; but while such an oversight is problematic, it does not render all, or even most, of Schuyler's observations on "race" and culture invalid.

Indeed, much has been made of Schuyler's unique stance. Recall that a year earlier, in 1925, Alain Locke had pronounced the African American folk as the black cultural vanguard. Beginning with Hughes's response to Schuyler, "The Negro Artist and the Racial Mountain," which argues for the primacy of racial positionality in poetry written by African Americans (the poet should be "interpreting the beauty of his own people,"[17] a theory of art assuming a community of "race") and continuing through the present day, Schuyler's position has been questioned as assimilationist, accommodationist, and counterproductive to the struggle for racial equality. Perhaps the phrase of Schuyler's that has caused the most alarm for critics and artists such as Hughes is the assertion that "the Aframerican is merely a lampblacked Anglo-Saxon."[18] Hughes claims that such a statement demonstrates "the desire to pour racial individuality into the mold of American standardization, and to be as little Negro and as much American as possible."[19] Even for a racial constructionist, such language can prove problematic, for after all, isn't Schuyler saying that all people are essentially white? Does this pronouncement deconstruct "race" or merely reconstruct a dominant whiteness?

I submit that one needs to consider several factors in deciphering Schuyler's comment. First, Schuyler is primarily a satirist, and in his writing, even his serious nonfiction, he is given to broad, bold, provocative statements. Schuyler has only the highest praise for writers "gifted in hyperbole and [whose] sarcasm was corroding."[20] Although we cannot attribute this assertion merely to a love of overstatement, we can take a second look at the cultural implications it has. Second, Schuyler's notion of the "lampblacked Anglo-Saxon" is doggedly amorphous in terms of what "racial" characteristics are, still allowing for the primacy of geography and class in the shaping of culture. That is, while Anglo-Saxon refers to an originary locus of whiteness in America, it is also a generality describing whiteness in its grossest terms but refusing to pin down the parameters of that identity precisely. Anglo-Saxon, as Schuyler employs the term both in this instance and in *Black No More,* is not a unifying category. Taking the novel as an example, difference within the white community is often as significant as difference among African Americans; in some respects, the takeover of government power in *Black No More* by avowed racist groups fails because these organizations find it impossible to define themselves simply in terms of whiteness to the exclusion of factors such as class. Although all factions are united in promoting racism, the Democratic Convention deadlocks over candidates because "one was too radical, another too conservative, a third was an atheist" (163), and so on through ten separate candidates. Recalling Balibar, Schuyler points to the ways in which a quest for "purity" in one area often exposes heterogeneity in others.

Third, the metaphor of the "lampblacked Anglo-Saxon" recalls both minstrelsy and—one of Schuyler's favorite topics—skin whiteners for African Americans. In terms of the latter, Schuyler's repeated and harsh criticisms of blacks who want to make themselves look more nordic or "pork-skinned" demonstrate that he did not believe that whiteness represents superior, or more essential, humanity.[21] In terms of outward appearance, Schuyler states that "Negroes possess within their group the most handsome people in the United States. . . . the percentage of beautiful folk is unquestionably larger than among the ofay brethren."[22] Black is beautiful for Schuyler, and even more civilized: "The Aframerican, being more tolerant than the Caucasian, is ready to admit that all white people are not the same."[23] In this satiric reversal of a racist cliché, Schuyler suggests the fallacy of color-culture links. He also discusses how class distinctions supersede those of "race," writing that

> practically every member of the Negro aristocracy . . . has worked at one time or another for white folks and observed with cynical detachment their orgies, obsessions and imbecilities, while contact with the white proletariat has acquainted him thoroughly with their gross stupidity and often very evident inferiority.[24]

While such a statement reveals class bias and bigotry in its own right, it is also important because it moves to recast the racial hierarchy in American society. In replacing the "supremacy" of whiteness with that of bourgeois blackness, Schuyler points to the way class and race combine in racialist hegemony to signify levels of difference. His insistence on superiority, however, lends the impression of unbridgeable racial gaps. Although problematic, such a formulation brings the discussion to a new level of complexity. If we apply the notion of "lampblack" to this statement, these new qualitative distinctions begin to deconstruct themselves. Indeed, the metaphor of the "lampblacked Anglo-Saxon" is meant to suggest the arbitrary nature of color and culture rather than the subordination of one color to another.

With respect to minstrelsy, the image of the lampblacked Anglo-Saxon has even more powerful resonances for Schuyler's theory of "race." Minstrelsy suggests at its root that "race" is performable, if not always already performed. That is, with the proper makeup, a white person could be "black," and by removing pigmentation, a black person could become "white." "Race" is theatrical—it is an outward spectacle—rather than being anything internal or essential. This is not to discount the gravity of internalized racism that I mentioned earlier, but it does point to even that as a learned pattern of behavior. Almost any performance can be repeated to the point of seeming essential, but there still remains the possibility of alternative performances. If racism is internalized, that does not mean that the internalizer must *always* enact his or her "inferiority." What Schuyler implies is that one adopts positions and learned behaviors thought to be specifically "racial," rather than deriving ethnic, "colored," or cultural identity from some sort of intangible racial spirit. Further, Schuyler implies that poets who write themselves into a conception of African American folk are engaged in an act based on the chimera of racial likeness if their own background does not correspond to the folk; they are African Americans participating in a unique type of minstrelsy. Like their associates busy whitening their skins, they are attempting to be something they are not. The upshot of all this is that being of one "race" or another is more a matter of conscious thought than genetic phenotype.

What Schuyler does here is create space for competing discourses of black identity; he attempts to make room for a variety of blacknesses to exist at once, leaving questions of authenticity to individuals' performative decisions. Hughes's reply to "The Negro-Art Hokum" is instructive, however, in that it voices concern that such a diverse range of discourses could lead to the destruction of blackness at the expense of dominant whiteness; he reasons syllogistically that the utterance "I want to be a poet—not a Negro poet" may actually mean "I would like to be white."[25] Of course, as Schuyler himself would probably suggest, the former phrase is not a denial of skin color but a denial of race constructed as folk (and Hughes locates the speaker of these lines as a member of the black bourgeoisie), of color constructed as culture. Hughes goes on from this opening paragraph further to critique the black bourgeoisie, equating middle-class status with a distance from "the eternal tom-tom beating in the Negro soul."[26] Authentic culture, for Hughes, is color based, innately soul driven, and it is the primacy of that discourse that Schuyler attempts to unravel in his work. Schuyler hears no tom-toms in his hometown of Syracuse, New York, nor does he find them an integral part of a specifically American black identity. Ultimately, Schuyler seeks to devise a theory of "race" and a corresponding aesthetic that free him from a limiting subject position of the primitive "other" escaped somehow from the heart of darkness.

In fairness, however, the historical and sociological reality of Schuyler's position of black-white nondifference in "The Negro-Art Hokum" is questionable. Harry Williams points out that

> Schuyler exaggerated in stating the Negro's response to life in America was identical to the white's. Were that the case then American whites would have invented jazz and the blues, the "dozens" and "rapping." These "race" artistic products may also be "class" or regional art, but because black creativity was involved . . . they were black art.[27]

Williams is right to suggest that color does figure into one's experience in a racialist society. As a result of segregation and separation from "real" American (white) culture, new cultural forms and practices continue to develop within communities delineated by race. Schuyler's claim of the "lampblacked Anglo-Saxon" refuses to take into account the difference that lampblack can make. As much as being a makeup applied from the outside and readily recognizable as a "surface" that covers some other "reality" beneath its pigment, the lampblack has a profound effect on those who view it from the outside. As Walter White implies when he writes that African Americans "are never allowed to forget their race," external appearance does make a difference.[28] The difference color makes is not merely superficial with respect to many forms of cultural practice and production. As much as we may all "be the same underneath," Schuyler never fully addresses the implications of appearance and its potential as the basis of diverging cultural traditions. Racial categorization—the imposition of status from an external source or audience—works in concert with a performative discourse of identity to shape the range of possible "authenticities." It is in considering this range, however, that despite his flaws, Schuyler makes a great contribution to the debate over both African American and American identity. In demystifying "natural" markers of identity, Schuyler lays a framework for subversion and reinvention. The import of much of Schuyler's work is to open up discursive space where culture and color are freed from certain connections and reattached to others. Schuyler is interested in bringing multiple subject positions to the African American individual, thereby offering liberating possibilities within American politics and culture, rather than reproducing naturalized, oppressive, and exclusive notions of "race" in the name of independence.

## Colorless Culture

Let us explore, then, the consequences of Schuyler's extreme position of colorless culture in the context of *Black No More*. As Schuyler backs away from skin color and relies more heavily on class, geography, and gender as markers of cultural identity and shapers of cultural activity, what happens to the notion of "race" that sets the action of the novel in motion in the first place? Harry Williams writes that "the primary theme of *Black No More* is the destructiveness and foolishness of America's obsession with skin color."[29] In dissecting the "foolishness" of color as the primary mark of identity, then, how does one distinguish like from different, friend from foe?

Right from the outset of *Black No More,* Schuyler questions markers of racial "reality" and "authenticity." When Crookman's investors question the efficacy of the Black-No-More treatment because though it changes appearance, it cannot change behaviors, he responds: "There is no such thing as Negro dialect, except in literature and drama. It is a well-known fact among informed persons that a Negro from a given section speaks the same dialect as his white neighbors. . . . There are no racial or color dialects; only sectional dialects" (31). In this moment, Schuyler stakes the entire success of Crookman's (and his own) project on de-essentialized notions of "race."[30] By displacing racial "reality" onto geographic location, Schuyler takes the bold step of examining constructs of color, rather than color in and of itself, as determinants of power relationships in the United States. Although this particular formulation seems to ignore a difference that "race" can make, it is important to the revisionary project at hand. In this move, reinscribing difference in alternative terms rather than positing color as prescriptive, Schuyler estimates a need to reassess how language can be employed to create hierarchies of difference. Whereas Crookman's reasoning is, indeed, loose with respect to dialects of Black English and the existence of their speakers, the wider significance of the passage is to examine the space where "standard" and "nonstandard" break down because they are presented as racial characteristics.

On another level, Schuyler also points to "race" as something performed rather than something intrinsic. Crookman's reference to literature and drama is instructive in the sense that they point to "race" not only as a fictional construct but also as a category that is necessarily invoked, controlled, and codified in specific ways to elicit specific responses from an audience. Through his process, however, Crookman disrupts the concept of authenticity. "Race" is transformed from a steady, knowable (through repeated performance) entity to an avant-garde, unknowable, and subversive act. That is, "race," after undergoing the Crookman treatment, begins losing its power to signify difference and thus jeopardizes the racialist social fabric of the United States.

Further defamiliarizing his readers with the notion of color as culture, Schuyler, toward the end of the novel, puts the following words into the mouth of the Knights of Nordica leader Givens: "Yes, Bunny . . . I guess we're all niggers now" (193). Givens's use of language proves particularly insightful because while on the one hand it maintains a notion of color as culture—he only says this because he finds out about his African American ancestors—on the other it shows the fluid possibilities of classification and identity. Static, narrow definitions leave themselves open to critique through the rigid concepts of authenticity they impose; refusing the possibility of genetic "mixing" and cross-cultural similarities, they attempt to reify difference in a particularly fragile state. Imagine African Americans running the KKK! With a "one-drop" African American promoting some of the most insidious forms of racism, Schuyler points to the ludicrous extremes to which racial identity can be taken. Social categorization and identification by "race" become self-defeating propositions. Schuyler serves notice through Givens that even the behavior by which we judge black from white, the performance that signals "race," is at best an unstable category. If we reexamine performance in a new context, there may not be anything distinguishing about it at all.

Indeed, Schuyler, in writing commentary as well as fiction, has forcefully set forth the fictional script that serves as a guideline of (stereo)typical and "authentic" racial performance. Attacking the generalizing qualities of racial classification, Schuyler asserts that "the term Negro itself is as fictitious as the theory of white racial superiority on which Anglo-Saxon civilization is based. . . . [I]t facilitates acceptance of the fiction of similarity and identity which is easily translated into a policy of treating all colored people the same."[31] Certainly, Schuyler is not arguing for the actual physical absence of people with dark skins but rather attempting to deconstruct "race" as a template by which we can reduce the complexity of social formation and interaction to an easily knowable, distinguishable, and reproducible factor. By limiting the possible range of subject positions available, we perpetuate an oppressive structure.

Similarly, Schuyler goes after the essentializing nature of "racial" discourse as it applies to white as well as African Americans:

> As the distance between the poor whites and the rich whites widens, the ofay commonality will probably occupy a place in society not unlike that of their forebears in Dixie before Secession, with nothing to look forward to in life save the dubious distinction of being free, white and twenty-one. That satisfaction, however, is considerable when there is no other.[32]

In a discourse that employs "race" as its primary marker of difference, even the whites necessarily must—in an utterly fatuous manner—elide their internal differences, differences such as class that, were they to be fully explored, are in themselves enough to rock the foundation of white hegemony. Whiteness needs to be performed as antiblackness to maintain the status quo; class difference and its radical potential are consumed by the leviathan of race. In *Black No More*, Max/Matt recognizes and exploits this artificial race-based commonality. In solidifying his hold on the Knights of Nordica, Max/Matt engages in a cynical act of race baiting with respect to trade unions and their political potential for the proletariat. The narrator privileges us to Max/Matt's thoughts:

> The working people were far more interested in what they considered, or were told was, the larger issue of race. It did not matter that they had to send their children into the mills to augment the family wage; that they were always sickly and that their death rate was high. What mattered such little things when the very foundation of civilization, white supremacy, was threatened? (131)

The irony is clear. Schuyler invokes race as the common denominator among people when it is quite obvious that class and the relation to the mode of production are what primarily draw them together.[33]

The result of such a system for the characters of *Black No More* is an increased potential for subversion of the system once they undergo Crookman's process. Because class and geographic difference are not at the basis of the recognition of difference in the novel's world, Max/Matt and the other characters can slip undetected into the "whitest" bastions of white society. Matt/Max, for example, describes part of his sojourn as a "white" man in Atlanta as a "let-down . . . from the good breeding, sophistica-tion, refinement and gentle cynicism to which he had become accustomed as a popular young man about town in New York's Black Belt" (64). By becoming white, he "steps down" class-wise in certain circles, yet that difference is overlooked because of whiteness. As an outsider, Max/Matt recognizes the primacy of color over class in this particular discourse, and this is why he is able to cement a political bond between the aris-tocratic Snobbcraft and "white trash" Givens. Such insight on the part of Max/Matt is a further method by which Schuyler depicts the power-ful notion of color as culture while simultaneously dismantling it. If color were indeed culture, Max/Matt—who is only superficially white—should be easily discovered. His black essence should show through.

But since, for Schuyler at least, class and geography are the factors by which similarity and difference are best judged, Max/Matt does not merely blend into "white" culture but assumes a leadership role in it. His status as a northern "intellectual" lends him authority in the South. Max/Matt ironically uses his status as "a resident of New York City" (69) as his cre-dential to become an expert on the effects of Crookman's process, and his utterly invented position as a member of the "New York Anthropo-logical Society" (67) to gain access to structures of power. In the North, Max/Matt "passes" with ease partially because "there are thousands of white people, yes millions, who look like" he does (39) and because in a racialist society, particularly in a metropolis such as New York, the belief in color as culture blinds much of the audience to potential "failures" in Max/Matt's performance. On another level, within whiteness itself, there are a multitude of performable subject positions, thereby making it some-what more difficult for the "passer" to be discovered. Even among his African American friends, Max/Matt can "pass" successfully. When he ap-proaches his old hangout after undergoing the process, he is told to "go 'way f'm here, white man" (41), and only when Bunny sees "the same sar-donic twinkle—so characteristic of his friend" (42) is Max/Matt's "true" identity recognized.

Max/Matt's distinctive physical performance is the only thing that gives him away, since African Americans, too, see color as culture and the primary means to "know" somebody ("The voice was Max Disher's, but the man was still white," thinks Bunny [42]). Finally Max/Matt seems to be able to extend his performance at will only by taking care publicly not to perform any behavior that might be perceived as African American. He tells the newly whitened Bunny, for instance, to "hold that race stuff, you're not a shine anymore" (115). Only by reinserting themselves in a specifically "racial" context can they be discovered. There is no need for Max/Matt to "train" to be white because he already perfectly understands his position and power in terms of class and language. Culture must be colorless, despite its division along the color line, for Max/Matt's "infiltration" to take place.[34]

Although Max/Matt's colorless bourgeois identity allows him to infiltrate the white power structure, and his geographic roots in the South give him insight into the particular workings of "race" in the region and the Knights of Nordica, we must not ignore his motivation for undergoing Crookman's treatment and beginning this odyssey into performative black-white identity in the first place. Before Crookman, before Atlanta, before Givens, and before politics, there was Helen. It is in search of her that Max/Matt begins his trek into whiteness, and it is significant that in Helen, Schuyler places a nexus of difference, sexual desire, and the motivation for social sabotage. On a self-conscious literary level, Schuyler is taking aim at Homer and one of the "foundational texts" of Western civilization; through this parody, Schuyler lays claim to and modifies yet another marker of whiteness and its supposed cultural superiority. One of the few female characters in *Black No More,* Helen occupies a central, albeit mainly symbolic, position within the text.

When phenotypically black men, Max/Matt and Bunny discuss their desire for, and opinions of, various sorts of women ("yallah," black, etc.), it could be a scene directly from Wallace Thurman's *The Blacker the Berry.* When Helen appears in the nightclub where the two friends sit, Bunny exclaims, "Now that's my speed" (20), but Max/Matt proclaims her unknowability across the color line, stating, "you couldn't touch her with a forty-foot pole," his opinion underscored by his ability to "tell a cracker a block away" (20). Max/Matt's statement serves as a marker of how cultural norms of (hetero)sexuality are delineated along racial lines. The regulation of black male desire stands as a means of maintaining difference, the unknowability of Helen maintaining the "purity" of the races. When Max/Matt does approach her for a dance, Helen replies, "I never dance with niggers! . . . Can you beat the nerve of these darkies?" (23), reinforcing Max's observations on color and providing a challenge for the protagonist to overcome. Schuyler introduces color as an apparently insurmountable difference along with the desire *for* difference, a concept to which he returns later in the text to make his theory of learned and performed "race" even more complex.

In figuring difference as desire, Schuyler raises important issues of the roles gender and sexuality play in configuring "race." Hazel Carby, in her commentary on the cult of true womanhood within the white southern social structure, suggests that to be a "true" woman, "the possession of virtue was imperative."[35] Performing this part admirably (though Schuyler assures us that it is strictly performance), Helen stands, in some ways, as a parody of this construct. Although she plays the role of virtuous maiden, Schuyler makes a point that her finishing-school education has resulted in a loss of "both her provincialism and her chastity" (75), the point being not to impugn Helen's morality as such, but rather to demonstrate the disparity between "ideal" white femininity and the particular case of Helen, who is held up as an ideal example.

Virtue and chastity, however, are not foremost in Max/Matt's mind. He is consumed with desire for whiteness, a symptom of the internalized racism I mentioned earlier, but also a significant marker of Schuyler's own take on "race" and sexuality in the United States.[36] The whole premise of *Black No More* rests on the assertion that there are few, if any, "white" people in the United States who can claim to be "purely" white. That is, there has been more than just interracial desire going on; one doesn't arrive at Schuyler's dedication "to all Caucasians in the great republic who can trace their ancestry back ten generations and confidently assert that there are no Black leaves, twigs, limbs or branches on their family tree" without acknowledging the consummation of that desire.

Again Schuyler makes a brazen assertion although the evidence to back it up is inconclusive at best. At the same time, however, it points to an important confluence of issues: passing, miscegenation, and racial authenticity. Joel Williamson cites studies showing that just between 1900 and 1925, each year anywhere between 10,000 and 15,000 African Americans "defected from the Negro world and were then living, with their progeny, among whites."[37] Further, Gunnar Myrdal agrees with Melville Herskovitz that approximately 70 percent of African Americans have some admixture of white blood and that interracial sexual relationships occurred "rather freely" in the seventeenth century while subsequent anti-miscegenation laws "probably did not diminish their occurrence in any appreciable degree"—though he also asserts that "the effect of passing on the American *white* population can never become important . . . because the numbers who pass are insignificant compared to the huge American white population."[38] In contrast, James Johnston asserts the rather commonplace status, during the colonial period, of a " 'white' wife of a white citizen of Virginia . . . [who] 'did not know whether she was entirely white or not.' "[39]

Most of these studies are concerned with the "dilution" of blackness rather than the "pollution" of whiteness, but I think that Myrdal's rather defensive position regarding the relative "purity" of whiteness (despite his assertion of a great deal of race mixing among African Americans) reflects a discourse unwilling to acknowledge the possibility of widespread miscegenation. Indeed, a one-drop hegemony would necessitate such myopia on the one hand while the whole object of passing "successfully" would serve to silence any admissions of (or even investigations into) biological blackness on the other. Although none of these studies focuses on African Americans in "white" family trees, the possibility seems very real, particularly for those white Americans not recently immigrated, that there could be one person of African descent among each of their 1,024 great-great-great-great-great-great-great-great grandparents (Schuyler's ten generations). In setting up such a scenario, Schuyler employs reductio ad absurdum against ideas of "one-drop" racial purity; miscegenation does not have to be the norm for it to have a profound effect on a racialist society.

Not content with the possibility of merely "remote" relationships between black and white, Schuyler makes the bold—and necessary for the novel, though perhaps overstated in "reality"—assertion that the urge for difference is the normative condition of sexual desire in the United States. Bunny, at the end of the novel, strikes up a relationship with an African American woman who has not undergone Crookman's process. Although Bunny calls her "a race patriot" (195), there is little evidence that he is attracted to her philosophical and intellectual understanding of the "race" issue. Rather, his exchange with Max/Matt mirrors quite closely their discussion of Helen at the beginning of *Black No More;* the now "white" Bunny desires difference (his "Sweet Georgia Brown" [195]) as much now as he did when he was black.

Although this particular assertion of the desire for difference is bound to cause outrage on either side of the color line—from African Americans who abhor it as an accommodationist omission of the systematized rape of black women and lynching of black men, to whites who would not want their daughters to marry one—Schuyler consistently maintains this position throughout his career. He does so not in an effort to deny an African American past he is well aware of (Max/Matt, even—indeed, especially— as a "white" man, has a nightmare that involves Helen and lynching [24]) but to continue his project of challenging and denaturalizing "race" as a stable governing concept. In advocating miscegenation, Schuyler is attempting to dismantle the color line itself; in 1930, a year before the publication of *Black No More,* Schuyler writes: "By 2000 A.D. a full-blooded American Negro may be rare enough to get a job in a museum, and a century from now our American social leaders may be as tanned naturally as they are now striving to become artificially."[40] That is, if people openly follow the miscegenistic impulses that are clung to in private, the race problem could be solved by obliterating "race" as a concept of purity. "Race" and the sexual baggage it carries become the ultimate American aphrodisiac. By indulging in this desire, which Schuyler insists in *Black No More* crosses all race and gender lines, Americans will naturally undermine the biggest fictional, unnatural construct that holds back their civilization.

Schuyler's proposal is a radical one; the erasure of "race" through desire is to a certain extent similar to Helga's dilemma in *Quicksand,* though she, in Larsen's more realistic world, could not extricate herself from unsatisfactory discourses of "race" simply by seizing on and invoking discourses of desire. Indeed, the two are much too intertwined for one to serve as the "antidote" to the other. My point in this comparison, however, is that a discursive racial community is maintained, at least in part, by the regulation of sexual desire while simultaneously those sexual practices "dangerous" to community are produced by that very regulation. The intersections of race and sexuality mark the bounds of community and contain within them the destruction of community. Schuyler's proposition to deregulate desire further points to the performed and nonessential nature of "race" itself. As Helga knows, racial-sexual roles are learned conventions;

Schuyler takes this knowledge and, in *Black No More,* subverts social order not only by changing physical appearance but also by undermining the language and ideology used to hold "racial" communities together.

Once the extent of miscegenation is revealed, white hegemony's language of race is an insufficient glue to hold together this newly reformulated "American" social fabric. Not only does the racist Givens proclaim, "we're all niggers now," but even established notions of racial performance lose their ability to mark and create difference. The destruction of the ideals of purity and authenticity mark, for Schuyler, the demise of "convenient propaganda devices to emphasize the great gulf which we are taught to believe exists between these groups of people."[41] Max/Matt employs "racial integrity talks [he thought] would click with the crackers" (117), only to have their preposterous nature demonstrated later on. Racial terminology is, by and large, voided of its meaning, and the script of racial performance needs necessarily be rewritten.

Ironically, the two characters most invested in ideals of (white) racial purity, Snobbcraft and his sidekick Buggerie, are first forced to acknowledge the performative nature of race and second perish at the hands of the essentialist hegemony they have created. After their African American ancestry is revealed, the two escape from the lynch mob beating at their doors; their plane crashes in the backwaters of Mississippi, and Snobbcraft and Buggerie are forced to don blackface in an effort save their own lives. Schuyler relishes the irony, having Buggerie proclaim, "If we take this blacking off we're lost. . . . With our pictures all over the country, it would be suicidal to turn up here in one of these hotbeds of bigotry and ignorance" (212). With their own backgrounds revealed, these proponents of racist essentialism are only too eager to embrace the possibility that nongenetic factors actually form the basis of "race."

Unfortunately for them, and gleefully for Schuyler, their impromptu minstrel show proves too convincing. Performing their blackness across the countryside, Snobbcraft and Buggerie meet up with the ultimate band of white racists and are threatened with lynching. Disavowing their performance, the two unmask themselves as "true" white men. However, their actual "impure" identities are revealed, and they are subsequently lynched anyway, with the mob's leader exclaiming, "They're niggers just as I thought. The Lord's will be done. Idea of niggers runnin' on th' Demmycratic ticket!" (216). Their own racist essentialism claims their lives, even as ex-black people stand in the mob and look on, performing their white-ness by "prod[ding] the burning bodies with sticks and cast[ing] stones at them. This exhibition restored them to favor and banished any suspicion that they might not be one-hundred-per-cent Americans" (218). While the rest of the nation becomes "definitely and enthusiastically mulatto-minded" (222), a symbol of the decline of the color line and its ideological, social, and linguistic support systems, essentialists prey on essentialists. Color as the ultimate definition of difference is exposed as the brutal and pernicious system that it is. Schuyler and his theory of race get the last laugh in the satire of *Black No More,* for no longer is "black" no more, but neither is "white."

Michael Peplow summarizes the major political concern of *Black No More* as the fear that "the disappearance of blacks will cause irreparable harm to the nation's political structure."[42] This is a fair synopsis of the novel's plot machinations, but Schuyler always implies an even greater goal of making not just "black" vanish, but "white," too. It is this disruption of hegemony based on any "race" that Schuyler seeks to accomplish. He explicitly challenges the "natural" order of race held by both black and white Americans. He defies his readers to think of "race" as an accurate and legitimate category of distinguishing between people.

In dissolving notions of culture based on color, Schuyler presents chal-lenges to both African and white Americans. In a system that trains us to think in terms of black and white, Schuyler's rather radical proposal that "the words 'Negro,' 'white,' 'Caucasian,' 'Nordic,' and 'Aryan' would have to be permanently taken out of circulation" if we are to begin solving the problem of racial discrimination leaves us stripped of familiar tools that we have used to explain our situations for years.[43] For Schuyler, an invo-cation of race is an invocation of race; we can hardly begin to dismantle this hegemony based on difference, by continually insisting on that dif-ference even though the use of "race" in terms of liberation may have a different emphasis than the use of "race" as an instrument of oppres-sion. The only way to break the felt twoness of double consciousness is to smash the race-based hegemony that necessitates this cultural schizophre-nia in African Americans. By insisting on authentic racial difference, we may be able to chip away at some aspects of hegemony, but we wind up reproducing it in other, unexpected ways.

Will race-based criticism that insists on certain figurations of black difference suffice when investigating an author who attempts to configure difference in alternate ways? Such criticism may provide some insight, since Schuyler—despite the claims of some detractors—was keenly interested in the place of the African American in the United States, but at the same time, it obscures some of his original and unconventional thinking. On the one hand, Schuyler may be wondered at as a "paradox," or "a raging, incomprehensible individualist."[44] On the other, he dreams of a world where " 'chromatic perfectionism' was temporarily achieved at the expense of a loss of individual integrity."[45] Indeed, Schuyler believes in the individual, and even a conservative meritocracy, but for him that individualism cannot be achieved through an individual integrity that equates with racial integrity, since "race" is an always already biased term.

Part of Schuyler's legacy is the way in which he establishes multiple, simultaneous, and "authentic" discourses as a way of understanding and undermining formulations of race. In doing so, he explodes old notions of blackness and debunks corresponding parasitic visions of whiteness. The upshot of this project in *Black No More* is to offer his readers a reinvented America one step beyond race consciousness and two steps beyond race hatred. His solution is by no means unproblematic; indeed, his insistence on the necessity of miscegenation contradicts his stance on the basically performative structure of "race." His position does point, however, toward a possible way of rethinking the dynamics of culture and race, suggesting a need to create cross-culturally without requiring one to repress the complicated baggage of gender, geography, class, and sexuality. Ultimately, Schuyler leaves us not with the question of whether to reimagine our communities and reinvent our traditions, but rather with the question of *how* we might do so. Perhaps in noting how, as Schuyler and others have pointed out, performative identity discourses exist in a matrix with one another, and also by recouping parts of "frontal assault" racial politics, we can arrive at an answer to this question.

The Possibilities

of Multiplicity:

Community,

Tradition, and

African American

Subject Positions

In describing some of the intersections of class, geography, gender, color, and "race," I hope it is apparent that "race" is, at best, an unstable entity open to subversion, appropriation, and conflicting interpretations at numerous political and literary moments. Seeking to define identity and delineate subjectivity in terms of "race," then, becomes a delicate enterprise, and building from unique representations of individual identity toward notions of racial communities and racial-cultural tradition presents an even more difficult, less concrete task for artist and intellectual. To seek the universal in the particular, while perhaps a powerful tool in one sense, also runs the risk of squelching diversity while promoting it. "Community" is both an empowering and a limiting concept. Of course, notions of individual subjectivity do not simply determine the definition of a community; indeed, ideas of community have a profound effect on shaping subjectivity. Nor do I wish to imply that conceptions of "racial" communities are ineffectual phantasms.

Johnson, Toomer, Larsen, Schuyler, and others, in interrogating specific discourses of black identity, raise questions about the efficacy of "race" as a descriptive term for both individual and community, as well as a term—with all the hidden baggage it brings with it—by which one can judge cultural production.

By insisting on "race" as a performative, tractable, and malleable category, the four authors I have discussed at some length seek to redefine "race" as a significant, controllable literary trope rather than a deterministic, essentializing categorization. In doing so, they offer multiple narratives on the complexity of blackness in the United States, suggesting ways in which, through imagining more diverse communities even within those communities of "minority" status, we might move toward solving problems of racism and its concomitant problems of homophobia, sexism, classism, regionalism, and colorism, all of which are expressions of essentialist thought in their own rights. What these authors point to, even if they never "succeed" in its creation, is a redefinition of "race," not as a precise descriptive term but as a tool of aesthetic and political change. "Race" becomes one possible lever in the cultural work of dislodging stubborn and exclusive institutions and practices from their seemingly stable and natural positions.

In conceiving of racial identity as a trope (and by trope I mean both "a figure of speech [that] turn[s] aside the telling of a story"[1] and " 'figures of thought' . . . in which words are used in a way that effects a conspicuous change in their standard meaning"),[2] we might destabilize the notion of "blackness" as identity and, through subsequent redeployments of the trope, seek to expand the cultural and political boundaries that limit a notion such as "race." Indeed, it is no accident that in and near the time when a self-described New Negro Movement was being articulated, Johnson, Toomer, Larsen, and Schuyler investigated the stability of the term "Negro" itself. If blackness can be remade, modified from old to new forms, what components of identity form the basis of Negroness? More important, how are those components employed to maintain a hierarchical pattern of social and cultural difference? In challenging the stability of blackness (and whiteness), we can contest the discourses of culture built on problematic ideas of "race."

It is important here to recall Judith Butler's invaluable work on discourses of gender identity. She asserts that there is neither an "essence" that gender expresses or externalizes nor an objective ideal to which gender aspires, and because gender is not a fact, the various acts of gender create the idea of gender, and without those acts, there would be no gender at all.[3]

Butler describes a process in which the destabilizers of "race" also participate. The further implication of such a process, such an invocation of a trope of identity, is to move away from the reification of an "essential" split between center and margin. This is not simply a project limited to the first decades of the twentieth century. The debate over discourses of blackness and the scope of African American representation stretches from well before the Harlem Renaissance to contemporary African American writing and literary and cultural theory. Trey Ellis, for example, has put forth the idea of the "cultural mulatto" explicitly in his artistic manifesto "The New Black Aesthetic" (1989) and, more implicitly, in his novel *Platitudes* (1988) as one possible method for subverting boundaries of black and white cultures. In the vein of many of his Harlem Renaissance predecessors, Ellis insists on simultaneous, intricate, and difficult-to-categorize visions of blackness as a weapon of aesthetic and political reform.

If identity is indeed performative, blackness need not be primarily—or even inherently—marginal. In light of the performative, our mental map of the distance between center and margin can be revised. This is, in part, Ellis's aim when he describes the cultural mulatto, by "race" a black person, who

> educated by a multi-racial mix of cultures, can also navigate easily in the white world. And it is by and large this rapidly growing group of cultural mulattoes that fuel the NBA [New Black Aesthetic]. We no longer need to deny or suppress any part of our complicated and sometimes contradictory cultural baggage to please either white people or black.[4]

His formulation of identity resists description in terms of existing categories of "race" alone. Indeed, the boundaries between center and margin are necessarily permeable in Ellis's revision of the subject, suggesting an increased complexity and flexibility requisite for the study of cultural production.

Yet as bell hooks suggests, the margin, too, has an important place in the discourse of blackness. She describes the margin as "a central location for the production of counterhegemonic discourse" and "a site one stays in, clings to even, because it nourishes one's capacity to resist."[5] Hooks underscores the dangers of the marginalized cultural worker as a participant in the hegemonic, calling attention to "ways of knowing that would lead to estrangement, alienation, and, worse, assimilation and cooption" of counterhegemonic alternatives.[6] Although her stance would seem to contradict Ellis's emphasis on cultural mulattoism, it is important the we hold these two postulations of difference concurrently in our view. Both employ a geographical imperative in grounding their work: hooks locates the origin of her discourse in the poor African American section of "a small Kentucky town," and Ellis places his in "the predominantly white, middle and working-class suburbs around Ann Arbor, Michigan, and New Haven, Connecticut."[7] The challenge then becomes not to privilege one geography and its corresponding discourse as more authentic than the other, but to embrace that sort of intraracial difference in all its subversive potential. Together these perspectives can provide a one-two punch to hegemonic concepts of culture and identity as well as discriminatory institutions. Hooks jabs from the margins, persistently calling attention to racist, sexist hierarchies within American society, and Ellis follows from closer to the "center" with a critique and subversion of that same "hegemonic" culture he feels himself part of as a cultural mulatto. In this way, we work to avoid one of Schuyler's pitfalls, the assumption that exclusive cultural institutions are penetrable without a strong voice of critique from the excluded. Rather than viewing hooks's and Ellis's positions as dramatically opposed, we can, in granting the possibility of a wide range of African American subject positions, see them as complementary in the fight to reimagine community and reinvent cultural traditions.

Certainly such disruptive diversity is not just a product of the 1980s. Theodore Vincent, describing the partial mission of the African American press in the 1920s, points out that "featuring news and analysis of black protest was but one method of distinguishing the black from the white papers."[8] Vincent's characterization of one function of the African American press proves instructive; a method of distinguishing between the "racial" characteristics of a periodical is to examine its sympathy toward a critique of white racism. Blackness derives strength, as hooks asserts, from its position at the margins. Although a discourse of black identity may construct itself as an oppositional voice to white oppression, such positionality may also be proactive as well as reactive. Rather than allowing itself to be delineated by the centrality of whiteness in Western culture, an idea of "race" that views itself as a performative trope offers the possibility of infiltration into, and subversion of, white-privileging hegemony along with a critique from the margin itself.

Ellis, for example, negotiates and undermines the boundaries of "racial" margins by linking Eurocentric postmodernism to the Afrocentric trope of signifyin(g). He allows a culturally specific expression of marginalized blackness—a form in which the performer "dwells at the margins of discourse, ever punning, ever troping, ever embodying the ambiguities of language"[9]—to inform a hegemonic literary form that functions as a "self-conscious, self-contradictory, self-undermining statement . . . [whose] distinctive character lies in [a] kind of wholesale 'nudging' commitment to doubleness, or duplicity."[10] In balancing these forms in *Platitudes,* Ellis begins to break down "authentically racial" categories and repostulate the relationship between "racial" cultures. A struggle between Isshe Ayam, a feminist African American woman novelist who favors a vision of the "folk" as authentic, and Dewayne Wellington, a buppie, fledgling novelist, and protocultural mulatto who wishes to write about black bourgeois characters in the urban North, stands as the novel's central theme. The writers engage in hilarious literary combat over the "proper" representations of African Americans and the political impact such representations can have.

The running battle between Dewayne and Isshe encompasses more, however, than just "internal" African American disputes over representation; it also points to the ways in which African American cultural workers seek to reimagine a wider American community and reinvent U.S. cultural traditions. In parodying the (culturally biased?) PSAT by making a question read "The civil rights leader was _____ to believe the police officer when he said he 'liked the colored'" (the correct answer is "a. naive"), Ellis moves to infuse (white) American institutions with experience drawn from the margins.[11] More than critique, Ellis dares to co-opt and reinvent American tradition on his own terms. He engages a discourse of blackness that, as Henry Louis Gates Jr. reminds us,

arose in response to allegations of its absence. . . . The recording
of an authentic black voice—a voice of deliverance from the deafen-
ing discursive silence which enlightened Europe cited to prove the
absence of the African's humanity—was the millennial instrument
through which the African would become the European, the slave
the ex-slave, brute animal become the human being.[12]

But Ellis moves beyond these originary formulations of literary blackness
as a reactive means of countering claims of subhumanity, its terms always
already defined by whiteness or, more precisely, nonwhiteness. Ellis both
criticizes and ironically remakes the institution of the PSAT, and, in doing
so, places his ("racially" black) cultural mulatto at the center of one American discourse. In breaking from notions of authentically black or white
culture, Ellis suggests radical new possibilities for the use of "race." Although Dewayne and his northern bourgeois character Earle may be "inauthentic" in some particularly strict formulations of African American
identity, that "inauthenticity" also turns out to have a good deal of power
in its own right. If we recall Butler's critique of ideal gender, authenticity
becomes, at best, a repeated (and thereby "naturalized") performance,
and consequently repeated "inauthenticity" should be able to cause its
sustaining and defining opposite to collapse on itself. Performed authenticity carries its own destruction in its very makeup. Although center and
margin may sanction specific discourses as authentic, the drive toward
the depiction of racial difference actually, through its status as repetitious,
discursive act, demonstrates the constructed nature of racial difference,
thereby calling into question not only notions of authenticity but also
corresponding notions of stable, intrinsic communities themselves. The
*writing* of "race" is equally if not more significant than the writing of
"*race*"; that is, the practice of employing a trope of identity carries as
much weight as the specific makeup of the trope itself. There is no single,
best set of circumstances that manifest the fiction of "racial authenticity."
Rather, it is the process of representation that must become preeminent.

This is not to say that the specific makeup of various versions of "race"
identities has no relevance to the study and construction of literary blackness. On the contrary, unspoken links between class and "race"—blackness having a certain class status as a "requisite" component—allow the
narrator of *The Autobiography of an Ex-Colored Man* to explore the intrica-

cies of identity politics and cultural creativity. Similarly, the intersections of "race" and gender in Larsen's *Quicksand* are at the heart of examining the interdependence of two apparently distinct forms of oppression. On a wider level, however, the tropological nature of "race" challenges the entire notion of community itself. Performativity points not only toward Butler's absence of essence among individuals but also to the ultimately constructed, imagined, and performed status of "community" itself and its highly volatile relations to cultural identity and cultural production.

Benedict Anderson has described the concept of the nation as one of an "imagined community." Certainly a "race"-based community does not necessarily correspond to the idea of nation, but an examination of some parallels proves enlightening. Anderson asserts that "all communities larger than primordial villages of face-to-face contact (and perhaps even these) are imagined. Communities are to be distinguished, not by their falsity/genuineness, but by the style in which they are imagined."[13] Two elements here seem important for my consideration of racial discourse. First, Anderson's commentary on "genuineness" bespeaks, in some fashion, my own concerns about authenticity. To assert the "reality" of an imagined entity risks positing normative criteria for membership that are simply possibilities in a spectrum, thereby repressing heterogeneity vital to the growth and evolution of community. Second, if communities, like individual identities, are constructs of repeated and repeatable codes (Anderson's "style"), then delineating the discourses of community could yield valuable insight into its complex relationships to both individual identity and literary and cultural production. The study of codes of community can provide space for commentary on the politics of representation.

Anderson goes on to state that the concept of community is significant "because, regardless of the actual inequality and exploitation that may prevail in each, the nation is always conceived as a deep, horizontal comradeship."[14] Indeed, Anderson points to the idea of a united front or "brotherhood" that supersedes the individual in the creation of an apparently cohesive whole. I would suggest that this is related to the exteriorization of specific types of markers of identity authenticity. That is, the process of creating horizontal comradeship corresponds to the desire and ability of someone to write/perform herself or himself into a discourse of community and its discourses of individual identity. It is what allows Toomer's narrators—particularly Kabnis—to go south and situate themselves among the geographical folk in an effort to connect to a prevailing notion of "racial" identity. It is what Ellis's fictional novelist Dewayne is reacting against when he describes what Earle's mother "does not look like":

> She is neither fat (her breasts don't swell the lace top of the apron she has never owned), nor has she any gold teeth. She cannot sing, nor is she ever called "Mama." . . . She does not, not work in public relations and her two-handed backhand is not, not envied by her peers. (4)

As well as when we are given a list of Earle's favorite things, including "all kinds of tanks, Janey Rosenbloom, Cream of Wheat . . . Chef Boy-Ar-Dee . . . cowboy boots and hats . . . Slurpees . . . Christmas [not Kwanzaa] . . . not Lenox Avenue" (20). Dewayne is engaged in a sort of counteridentification with an imagined community that bespeaks cultural alternatives. Further, this process of imagining a community is at work when Dewayne rewrites his book in an effort to modify its critical reception within a folk-centered discourse of literary blackness. By recasting his characters more in the mold of the prevailing discourse of literary blackness, Dewayne prompts Isshe, the novel's internal authenticator of blackness, to revise her opinion of his work from being "puerile, misogynistic, disjointed and amateurish ejaculations . . . [that] defile the temple of black literature" (39) to a novel "now coming along rather well" (148). In this process of writing/performing oneself into a discourse of literary blackness, identity may be performed in the quest for Anderson's "horizontal comradeship" of the wider imagined community; by the same token, ideas about the "nature" of that community inform formulations of individual "authentic" identity. The relative ease with which Dewayne transforms both himself (from "underachieving middle-aged black male 'artist' " [79] to a writer who deserves "the highest possible recommendation" for publication [172]) and his characters in *Platitudes* demonstrates, however, that little of such "essence" exists in the discourse of "race" that it cannot be negotiated in a complex but eminently achievable fashion by breaking some habits of language and employing different ones.

On another level, Kwame Anthony Appiah puts forth a fascinating link between the individual, the community, and culture when he writes that "the regression to a crude notion of a distinctive racial subjectivity . . . ties into the older humanistic conception of 'culture' as the province of a privileged subjectivity, to which the artist gives an especially exalted expression."[15] To expand on Appiah, the creation of a privileged, more "authentic" subjectivity allows for a more "authentic" cultural creation. This in turn helps legitimate not only the creator's individual identity but also his or her status as a member of the wider community, for the imagined community has—to a certain extent—its imaginary boundaries set and legitimized by cultural production. Johnson's narrator, for example, is engaged in precisely this sort of complex interchange between community, culture, and individual identity in his explorations of ragtime and African American folk music. His relation to the music cements, in some ways, his relationship to a broad African American community, despite his position of class privilege; music as a point of reference can partially elide internal difference in the way in which Anderson described horizontal comradeship of the imagined community. The narrator's ability to perform (literally the music) as folk bestows on him a particular "authentic" cultural identity while that same performance—as well as his arrangements and transcriptions—establishes him as a "producer" of that culture. This process is external and conscious, although, as Appiah intimates, given a racialist, essentialist way of investigating discourses of culture and identity, one could easily move to characterize the process as internal, intuitive, and intrinsic.

It is through insisting on the exteriority of identity—individual, communal, and cultural—however, that Johnson, Toomer, Larsen, and Schuyler make significant contributions to the creation and critique of discourses of authentic blackness. They, in the words of Cornel West, work to

> constitute and sustain discursive . . . networks that deconstruct earlier modern Black strategies for identity-formation, demystify power relations that incorporate class, patriarchal and homophobic biases, and construct more multi-valent and multi-dimensional responses that articulate the complexity and diversity of Black practices in the modern and postmodern world.[16]

African American identity becomes more than just a reactive invocation against racist, hegemonist declarations of its inferiority, though none of these writers goes so far as wholly to abandon marginality and the possible benefits within it. Indeed, these writers seem to anticipate Frantz Fanon's claim that "no colonial system draws its justification from the fact that the territories it dominates are culturally non-existent. You will never make colonialism blush for shame by spreading out little-known cultural treasures under its eyes."[17] Engaging marginalized folk culture and celebrating its forms insufficiently disrupts entrenched notions of identity and hierarchy; the valorization of folk strength still caters to and derives in part from African American marginality in a way that is effective as a voice of protest but not necessarily one of revision or revolution. Although the cultural treasures of African Americans, particularly those of folk derivation, play a key role in the formation of African American identity discourse, might we be better served to work at denaturalizing not only notions of African American identity and culture but also a general sense of American culture and identity?

Albert Barnes suggests that "what our prosaic civilization needs most is precisely the poetry which the average Negro lives."[18] From the context of the "New Negro," Barnes makes a leap to a "New American." Ellis modifies this idea—based on a notion of the "folk"—by offering the cultural mulatto as the vehicle by which to revitalize American culture. More than simply substituting one "authenticity" for another in an effort to describe a cultural vanguard, Ellis moves to place "an attitude of liberalism rather than a restrictive code" into the discourse of black identity.[19] By suggesting the reformative power of multiple authenticities, he hopes to make more difficult the reinscription of blackness as primarily marginal. In reimagining, reperforming, and reinventing concepts of African American community, identity, and culture, a number of black writers necessarily begin challenging notions of American identity, nation, and culture generally. In denaturalizing the distinctions between the two, authors can begin to lay the groundwork for community, culture, and identities constructed on new principles aware of the pitfalls of "that talk of the Afro-American experience [that] treats the complex worlds of millions of men and women as homogeneous, and thus treats black people as particularized expressions of racial essence."[20]

In eschewing those discourses of blackness, one can also subvert the discourses of American-ness that employ blackness as a reference point, picking apart "specific ways in which 'Whiteness' is a politically constructed category parasitic on 'Blackness.'"[21] As Schuyler suggests in *Black No More*, the ease with which cultural markers of "race" may be dropped or adopted certainly suggests the possibility (and perhaps even the necessity) of abandoning clear-cut notions of "race" for a chorus of multiple subject positions that more accurately reflect the complexity and diversity of constituent populations. Through the constant invocation of certain class, gender, geographic, and color imperatives, Johnson, Toomer, Larsen, and Schuyler have moved toward a discourse that destabilizes any one of those factors as the ultimate determinant of identity, community, and culture. In doing so, they invite their readers to rethink their notions of "history," at least in the sense of history as a narrative of collective identity, since as Eric Hobsbawm points out, "all invented traditions, so far as possible, use history as a legitimator of action and a cement of group cohesion."[22]

In contrast to a nascent form of cultural nationalism encoded in a collection such as Locke's *The New Negro,* these authors, in consistently reminding their readers of the performative, exterior construction of identity, resist "the overdetermined course of cultural nationalism . . . [the effect of which has been] to make real the imaginary identities to which Europe has subjected us."[23] I repeat this sentiment here not to impugn cultural nationalisms as movements in their own right (West correctly points to the need for "affirming and enabling subcultures of criticism," and Ellis claims his New Black Aesthetic "stems straight from that tradition" of nationalist pride)[24] but to offer a framework against which performative, tropological identity functions. If racial-cultural identity is derivative of, or assimilable into, hegemonic conceptions of both blackness and whiteness, performative identity offers another option by postulating alternative identities and cultures that not only are more difficult to categorize and subsume into hegemony but also, in their performativity, demonstrate the imagined and possibly tenuous status of constructed, denaturalized hegemony itself.

In beginning to propose a discourse of identity that discounts the inherent stability of racial identity as a precisely descriptive term, African American authors offer the first hints of a radical reformulation of discourse and reinvention of the black tradition. In writing themselves into an extant discourse of literary blackness, they embrace at strategic political moments "certain values and norms of behaviour [marked] by repetition, which automatically impl[y] continuity with the past."[25] That is, they align themselves with a version of African American history engaged in humanizing blackness, dismantling the (white) hegemonic discourse of blackness as animalistic and without history, and critiquing racism gen-

erally. Yet in insisting on the performativity of African American identity, they further challenge the assumptions of stability of both whiteness
and blackness. Recognizing the inherently oxymoronic status of any pur-
ported "authentic representation," they turn the process of representation
to the advantage of demystification. Following the logic of Butler,

> if rules governing signification [of identity] not only restrict, but
> enable the assertion of alternative domains of cultural intelligibility,
> i.e. new possibilities for gender that contest the rigid codes of hier-
> archical binarisms, then it is only *within* the practices of repetitive
> signifying that a subversion of identity becomes possible.[26]

We can, I believe, say much the same about race. When Johnson's narrator
and Helga Crane participate in ready-made discourses of blackness, they
expose the inadequacies of those discourses. Indeed, they can repeat the
actions that "create" blackness, but in that repetition, they shut out other
parts of the psyches, interests, and abilities. At the same time, however,
African American authors may also challenge the whiteness that reifies
blackness as its opposite. One of the great ironies of *The Autobiography
of an Ex-Colored Man* is that in spite of the narrator's musical composi-
tions that engage and reform African American cultural tradition, what
the reader is left with at the end of the book is, in many ways, a subversion of the discourse of whiteness. In leaving this "autobiography" as a
cultural text, one produced by a "white" (this is a large part of the significance of the phrase "ex-colored") man, Johnson's narrator dismantles
whiteness not only by pointing to the inherently paradoxical nature of
passing but also by having this "black" cultural text be produced, indeed enabled, by "white" culture, community, and identity. It appears
that if signified in a certain way, whiteness can indeed become a form
of blackness. Similarly, Schuyler's Knights of Nordica becomes an effective race-terror organization because its new leader—the black-no-more
Max/Matt—recognizes precisely which performances to emphasize in an
effort to call forth "white power," a knowledge he acquired by performing within a discourse of blackness on which whiteness depends. Indeed,
it appears difficult to reconstruct blackness through an emphasis on the
performative without affecting whiteness. The opposites are inseparable.
   This Butlerian emphasis on subversion and assertion of alternative cultural domains in effect requires its participants to reimagine their com-

munities. Within this reimagination is implicitly a critique of the old (or current) hegemonic order as well as cultural alternatives already available. This contributes to the "newness" of the New Negro and the New Black Aesthetic. Such a reimagination not only begins to recognize "the extraordinary diversity of subject positions, social experiences and cultural identities which compose the category 'black'" but, in doing much the same work for the category "white," causes us to rethink ways in which we "can effectively draw the political boundary lines without which political contestation is impossible, without fixing those boundaries for eternity."[27] Indeed, the concept of "community" can be reimagined in fluidity rather than fixity, as can invented cultural tradition itself.[28]

In this process of repoliticization, the denaturalization and decentralization of race, gender, class, sexuality, and geography become paramount. In the new paradigm(s), none of these is sufficient, in and of itself, to serve as a marker of community, tradition, or identity. On the contrary, it is the intersections of these various aspects that will have to function as guideposts in culture and politics, not as a "homogenous unity or monolithic totality but rather [as] a contingent, fragile coalition building in an effort to pursue common radical libertarian and democratic goals that overlap."[29] Indeed, I can only reemphasize the delicate constitution of such coalition politics; given the performative construction of its constituent parts, it is an always changing—or at least changeable—coalition. The "trick" for author, critic, and reader is to hold in place simultaneously as many of the constitutive variables as possible. In doing so, he or she exposes the delicate confederation of ideas on which various oppressions are based. Recognizing those intersections opens new possibilities in the struggle against those forms of subjugation.

Through an emphasis on the performative, I hope I point to a wider version of "race" and its politics. No longer can it suffice to talk about "race" as a term unproblematic in its own right; in deconstructing imagined communities and invented traditions centered on "race," we begin to recognize the intersections of that term with equally important markers of "otherness." In speaking of "race/class/gender politics," the appreciation of the fact that these three terms are often promoted as a triad is edifying. On one level, such an invocation calls attention to the connectedness of these facets of identity, in this way, perhaps, expanding the boundaries of any one of the terms. In widening the base of the discourse of "race" through careful attention of the workings of class and gender, for example, we can come to a greater understanding of the subtleties of racism and, through that knowledge, attempt to subvert it. And as writers as diverse as Fanon, Hall, and Appiah have suggested, a more sophisticated look at "race" can even aid in reformulating policies of antiracism in terms even more subversive to hegemonic discourses of identity than those already in use.

On another level, however, racism is different from sexism is different from classism. Although all these forms of discrimination may function syncretically on and in an individual or community, we must take care to distinguish one from another in an effort to explicate more fully the workings of any one. Indeed, thinkers such as Butler and Patrick Joyce (who described class-based community in late-nineteenth and early-twentieth-century England as "built up out of the often ill-fitting bricks of . . . distinctive local and regional experiences, in which the parochial and the sectional were often finely balanced with the catholic and solidaristic")[30] have theorized issues of gender and class (relatively) independently of their "companion" markers of identity. This is not necessarily a fault on their parts, but rather a rethinking of the particular. To be sure, it is through the careful examination of the particular that many intellectuals—such as the novelists discussed in this book—can come to see the complexity of the issues at hand as well as the limitations of unique discourses, both hegemonic and oppositional.

All this is to say that the examination of "race" and racism is of extreme importance, even though "race" itself can be shown to be a cultural construction. The goal in discussing "race" in terms of the performative is not to close "race" out as a category of intellectual inquiry or social practice but to examine more closely the ways in which we employ that selfsame term in opposition to hegemonic racism. The performative gives us a view to the politics of representation, the intricate workings of intersecting discourses of identity, community, and culture, rather than a retreat into a sometimes useful but overly deterministic "propagandistic positivism" designed to reveal misrepresentations but also having the effect of perpetuating prescriptive notions of identity.[31]

Further, part of the significance of Johnson, Toomer, Larsen, and Schuyler is that their disputations of particular aspects of "racial" identity point out an interesting aspect of cultural and intellectual movements themselves. The New Negro Movement may embody, on one hand, "the African-consciousness of the writers who were part of the Harlem Renaissance."[32] In the sense that it offers alternative discourses of identity, culture, and community readily distinguishable from and radically revisionary with regard to the "Old Negro" and white-imposed and sanctioned discourses, the Harlem Renaissance also incorporates a critique of the "race" on which it was based, and in this self-critique, a good deal of subversion and opposition can also be found. In dismantling race via class, geography, gender, and assumptions about color and culture, these four authors demonstrate the pitfalls of oppositional thinking that has become "traditional." Where the folk-based New Negro challenged older formulations of "race," its vision was in turn challenged by critiques of its own narrowness. Along similar lines, *Platitudes* and the New Black Aesthetic reevaluate contemporary discourses of black identity that help us to read African American culture today; the process of critique and reform still goes on. Indeed, the value of "race" as an oppositional categorization and identification is perhaps even more hotly debated than ever.

The value of a performative, tropological employment of "race," however, is precisely the ability of the performer to be at once "inside" and "outside" racial discourse, both "really" black and not "black" at all. It is this sort of disruption, this ability to shift our various identities to highlight specific complexities and problems, that offers a great hope in working to dismantle racism, an ideology and practice based on always already untenable assumptions. As performativity reveals the mystified, naturalized, and constructed nature of those assumptions, we can move closer—in conjunction with similar theorists of class, geography, and gender—toward debunking the hierarchies keeping discriminatory practices in place. Further, critique must merge with wider reimagined communities in laying the foundation for change. As Ellis proclaims in his manifesto, "in the Twenties blacks wanted to be considered as good as dominant culture. . . . Today the NBA wants to dominate it."[33] In performativity and the reinventions it stimulates arises the possibility of radical, positive, more egalitarian social orders. Rather than remaining a reifying descriptive term, identity can become a tool in this metamorphosis. It is within the context of these reimagined communities, reinvented traditions, and alternative cultures that existing institutions themselves can be more easily (and necessarily) reformed.

Of course, via my own logic, even these reforms will eventually become hegemonic and meet with challenging alternatives. So be it. The process of creating culture(s) is ongoing, dynamic, and evolutionary. I hope my approach has been sensitive to that formulation. I have purposely avoided positing a grand unified theory of "race," identity, and culture because I do not think that to offer one would be particularly helpful. It could suggest an intriguing, though fleeting, model for action, but such a theory would also begin to collapse under the weight of its own imposed authenticity. I have chosen texts that "fail" in certain ways—Johnson's in its retreat into essence, Toomer's in its gender bias, Larsen's in its determinism, Schuyler's in its eugenics—to demonstrate fully the disruptive powers of the performativity these books have at their center. None anticipates the intersections of all the performative aspects that contribute to a notion of identity, and in failing to do so, each remains problematic in certain respects. Perhaps this is because the "perfect" performative text is as elusive as the "great American novel" or the Platonic form. This is why coalition politics are necessary; one member can pick up where another falls short. Through studying these particular texts in concert with one another, we can learn more about the discourses of black identity than from any one individually. This is a sort of coalition politics of reading I have attempted to engage. Do we really need a "grand unified theory" of black identity when comparing and contrasting a plurality of positions is immensely instructive in its own right? If it is through coalition and an empowerment of diversity that we are to come to the destruction of discrimination, let us begin that mission by creating the largest possible space in which coalitions may be formed and diversity displayed.

# Notes

## 1 Discourses of Black Identity: The Elements of Authenticity

1 Houston A. Baker Jr., *The Journey Back* (Chicago: University of Chicago Press, 1980), xii.

2 Houston A. Baker Jr., *Blues, Ideology, and Afro-American Literature: A Vernacular Theory* (Chicago: University of Chicago Press, 1984), 3.

3 Baker, *Blues,* 9.

4 Baker, *Blues,* 11.

5 The difference between "uniqueness," that which distinguishes, and "authenticity," that which privileges distinct features, lies herein: authenticity derives from uniqueness, but it also fixes that uniqueness to a limited range of possibilities. I contend that there are many "unique" forms of African American expression, but the critical fixation on "authentic" forms has generally kept them out of the field of intellectual inquiry. The authors I explore in depth in this study question the political, social, and literary value of authenticity by asserting, at strategic moments, unique expressions of blackness both counter to, and in line with, the discourse of authenticity.

6 Henry Louis Gates Jr., "Canon Formation, Literary History, and the Afro-American Tradition: From the Seen to the Told," in *Afro-American Literary Studies in the 1990's,* ed. Houston A. Baker Jr. and Patricia Redmond (Chicago: University of Chicago Press, 1989), 27.

7 Henry Louis Gates Jr., *Figures in Black* (New York: Oxford, 1987), 235–36.

8 Even my suggestion of "African American culture" here is problematic. It represents a slippage between the terms "race," as an essentialized, even biological concept, and "culture," as a social construction. Yet when we talk about "African American" or "black" culture, do we begin to conflate these two ideas? As my discussion of George Schuyler takes pains to point out, we must begin to question the boundaries we often too easily draw between cultures. I'm afraid that

a good deal of contemporary scholarship simply replaces the term "race" with "culture" without really considering the ever-shifting and evolving building blocks of the latter; such a linguistic substitution has the effect of renaturalizing notions of "race" rather than interrogating them. After all, to return to my own hypothetical, doesn't even a single nonblack raised in African American culture begin to modify the notion of what constitutes African American culture?

9 Etienne Balibar, "Paradoxes of Universality," trans. Michael Edwards, in *Anatomy of Racism,* ed. David Theo Goldberg (Minneapolis: University of Minnesota Press, 1990), 284–85.

10 Cornel West, *Race Matters* (New York: Vintage Books, 1993), 37.

11 West, *Race Matters,* 38–39.

12 Henry Louis Gates Jr., ed., "The Black Person in Art: How Should S/he Be Portrayed?" *Black American Literature Forum* 21, nos. 1–2 (spring–summer 1987): 3.

13 Michel Foucault, *The Archaeology of Knowledge,* trans. A. M. Sheridan Smith (New York: Harper and Row, 1972), 131.

14 Alain Locke, "The New Negro," in *The New Negro,* ed. Alain Locke (1925; New York: Atheneum, 1968), 6.

15 Alain Locke, "Negro Youth Speaks," in Locke, *The New Negro,* 48.

16 Locke, "Negro Youth Speaks," 48.

17 W. E. B. DuBois, "Criteria of Negro Art," *Crisis* 32 (October 1926): 290–97.

18 DuBois, "Criteria," 293.

19 W. E. B. DuBois, *The Souls of Black Folk* (1903; New York: Signet, 1969), 108.

20 Nathan I. Huggins, *Harlem Renaissance* (New York: Oxford, 1971), 19.

21 Locke, "The New Negro," 7.

22 Hazel V. Carby, "The Historical Novel of Slavery," in *Slavery and the Literary Imagination,* ed. Deborah E. McDowell and Arnold Rampersad (Baltimore: Johns Hopkins University Press, 1989), 127.

23 Barbara Smith, in Gates, "The Black Person in Art," 5.

24 E. Franklin Frazier, *Black Bourgeoisie* (New York: Free Press, 1957), 128.

25 Frazier, *Black Bourgeoisie,* 238.

26 Arthur Schomburg, "The Negro Digs Up His Past," in Locke, *The New Negro,* 231.

27 See Baker's *Blues, Ideology, and Afro-American Literature* for a contemporary version of this strain of thought. Baker's "economics of slavery" seems to me a direct descendant of Schomburg.

28 Schomburg, "Negro Digs Up His Past," 232.

29 Schomburg, "Negro Digs Up His Past," 237.

30 Wilson J. Moses, "The Lost World of the Negro, 1895–1919: Black Literary and Intellectual Life before the 'Renaissance,'" *Black American Literature Forum* 21, nos. 1–2 (spring–summer 1987): 76.

31 Moses, "Lost World," 78.

32  Huggins, *Harlem Renaissance*, 61.

33  Huggins, *Harlem Renaissance*, 61.

34  Nicholas Lemann, *The Promised Land: The Great Black Migration and How It Changed America* (New York: Knopf, 1991), 6.

35  Houston A. Baker Jr., *Modernism and the Harlem Renaissance* (Chicago: University of Chicago Press, 1987), 63.

36  Bernard W. Bell, *The Afro-American Novel and Its Traditions* (Amherst: University of Massachusetts Press, 1987), 94.

37  Huggins, *Harlem Renaissance*, 74–75.

38  By the same token, I find it interesting to note the type of critical attention given to Richard Wright's *Black Boy* as a text that embraces and derives its literary merit from the depiction of life among the African American folk. At the same time, however, *American Hunger*, the second part of Wright's autobiography, receives relatively little critical notice, perhaps because of its much more ambiguous stance toward folk culture, the folk, and the possibilities of building a harmonious culture around them.

39  David Levering Lewis, *When Harlem Was in Vogue* (New York: Oxford University Press, 1979), 124.

40  Perhaps one can most easily see these traits as "authentically white" in so-called mulatto literature. If one considers the characterization of the white parent (usually the father) in works such as Douglass's *Autobiography*, Johnson's *Autobiography of an Ex-Colored Man*, and Chesnutt's *Marrow of Tradition*, one notes that whiteness is often portrayed—though not necessarily exclusively—as avaricious and complicit with racial discrimination, even against one's own flesh and blood. The discourse of whiteness in African American literature is an area deserving of more study.

41  Lewis, *When Harlem Was in Vogue*, 95.

42  Feminist and womanist scholars have contributed significantly to the debate over the nature of black identity, and indeed I am heavily indebted to feminist scholarship and its work on the notions of identity and authenticity in general.

43  Huggins, *Harlem Renaissance*, 188.

44  Huggins, *Harlem Renaissance*, 7.

45  Huggins, *Harlem Renaissance*, 189.

46  John L. Hodge, "Equality: Beyond Dualism and Oppression," in Goldberg, *Anatomy of Racism*, 91.

47  Cheryl A. Wall, "Response to Kimberly W. Benston's 'Performing Blackness,'" in Baker and Redmond, *Afro-American Literary Studies*, 188. I should also like to note that Wall's assertion is not without some debate. David L. Smith has pointed me to some examples that might problematize Professor Wall's assertions about speechifying. I do not want here to engage in a discussion of precisely how African American public discourse is gendered at every particular

moment, though clearly the criticism of Anita Hill's public allegations against Clarence Thomas point to the need for further study of the ways in which public discourse is gendered and the consequences of that gendering. Rather, I include Professor Wall's remarks as an indication that we need to pay close attention to the ways in which African American discourses are not simply a matter of "race" or color.

48 Valerie Smith, "Black Feminist Theory," in *Changing Our Own Words,* ed. Cheryl A. Wall (New Brunswick: Rutgers University Press, 1989), 47.

49 Lucius Outlaw, "Toward a Critical Theory of 'Race,'" in Goldberg, *Anatomy of Racism,* 60.

50 Henry Louis Gates Jr., "Writing 'Race' and the Difference It Makes," in *"Race," Writing, and Difference,* ed. Henry Louis Gates Jr. (Chicago: University of Chicago Press, 1986), 5.

51 Werner Sollers, *Beyond Ethnicity* (New York: Oxford University Press, 1986), 31.

52 Judith Butler, "Gender Trouble, Feminist Theory, and Psychoanalytic Discourse," in *Feminism/Postmodernism,* ed. Linda J. Nicholson (New York: Routledge, 1990), 324.

53 Susan Bordo, "Feminism, Postmodernism, and Gender-Skepticism," in Nicholson, *Feminism/Postmodernism,* 137–38.

54 Outlaw, "Race," 77.

55 Gates, "Writing 'Race,'" 5.

56 Butler, "Gender Trouble," 337.

57 Baker, *Modernism,* 58.

58 Joel Williamson, *New People* (New York: Free Press, 1980), 164.

59 Baker, *Modernism,* 56.


2 *For a Mess of Pottage: James Weldon Johnson's Ex-Colored Man as (In)authentic Man*

1 Robert E. Fleming, *James Weldon Johnson and Arna Wendell Bontemps: A Reference Guide* (Boston: G. K. Hall, 1978), 6.

2 Bernard W. Bell, *The Afro-American Novel and Its Tradition* (Amherst: University of Massachusetts Press, 1987), 90–91.

3 Stephen H. Bronz, *Roots of Negro Racial Consciousness* (New York: Libra, 1964), 24.

4 Judith R. Berzon, *Neither White nor Black* (New York: New York University Press, 1978), 15.

5 Berzon, *Neither White nor Black,* 63.

6 Berzon also asserts some important connections between gender and racial authenticity. She describes "the all-but-white, usually female and beautiful character [who] titillatingly and effectively meets the specifications for successful

melodrama" and who figures prominently in what Berzon deems "mulatto fiction" (Berzon, *Neither White nor Black,* 13).

7   Eugene Levy, *James Weldon Johnson* (Chicago: University of Chicago Press, 1973), 66.

8   James Weldon Johnson, *Along This Way* (New York: Viking, 1933), 122.

9   Johnson, *Along This Way,* 122.

10  James Weldon Johnson, preface to *The Book of American Negro Poetry* (New York: Harcourt, Brace, 1922), vii.

11  John G. Mencke, *Mulattoes and Race Mixture: American Attitudes and Images* (Ann Arbor: UMI Research Press, 1979), 143.

12  bell hooks, *Black Looks* (Boston: South End Press, 1992), 10.

13  hooks, *Black Looks,* 9.

14  Johnson, *Along This Way,* 66.

15  Berzon, *Neither White nor Black,* 190.

16  Joel Williamson, *New People* (New York: Free Press, 1980), 130.

17  Johnson, preface to *American Negro Poetry,* xli.

18  Julian Mason, "James Weldon Johnson: A Southern Writer Resists the South," *CLA Journal* 31 (December 1987): 156.

19  Johnson, *Along This Way,* 31.

20  Zora Neale Hurston, *Their Eyes Were Watching God* (1937; New York: Perennial, 1990), 183.

21  There are several striking similarities between Johnson as historical figure and the narrator of *Ex-Colored Man,* not the least of which are several passages—related in the narrator's first-person voice—that Johnson takes from the novel and transplants wholesale into later works of nonfiction. And although one cannot make a one-to-one correlation between Johnson and the narrator, some of the latter's thoughts and experiences are undeniably formed by the former's own life. Johnson addresses this issue in an interesting fashion in his autobiography *Along This Way* (1933). He writes that *Ex-Colored Man* "was not the story of my life. Nevertheless, I continue to receive letters from persons . . . inquiring about this or that phase of my life as told in it. That is, probably, one of the reasons why I am writing the present book" (239). Although he denies that he is the novel's narrator, Johnson does not preclude all connection between his life and the text. Besides being an autobiographical record, *Along This Way* serves, in some small way, as a point of comparison for *Ex-Colored Man.*

22  I use the text of *The Autobiography of an Ex-Colored Man* found in *Three Negro Classics* (New York: Avon, 1965). All future page references to *Ex-Colored Man* will appear in the text.

23  Berzon, *Neither White nor Black,* 141.

24  Edward Byron Reuter, *The Mulatto in the United States* (Boston: Gorham Press, 1918), 315.

25  In a folk-privileging discourse of black identity, whiteness would be "antifolk." That is, white is what black is defining itself against, attempting to liberate itself from. Whiteness becomes defined as middle- or upper-class, educated, materialistic, individualistic, and so forth, precisely the types of traits E. Franklin Frazier suggested were a "world of make-believe" for black folks. From the perspective of a racist such as Reuter, we have already noted that whiteness connotes superior intellect, cultural tradition, morality, appearance, and economic status. Of course, both these constructions are as fallacious as the essentialization of blackness as the folk, yet they are parallel to one another. Both seek to define a homogeneous "race," with an eye toward establishing or solidifying a base of political power. Recall also that Balibar's concept of the paradox of universality derives from the study of *white* racist and nationalist thought and practice.

26  Bell, *Afro-American Novel*, 88.

27  Stuart Hall, "What Is This 'Black' in Black Popular Culture?" in *Black Popular Culture,* ed. Gina Dent (Seattle: Bay Press, 1992), 30.

28  This admiration of Shiny parallels, in some ways, Johnson's statement about Paul Laurence Dunbar as "an example at once refuting and confounding those who wish to believe that whatever extraordinary ability an Aframerican shows is due to an admixture of white blood" (preface to *American Negro Poetry*, xxxv). I point this out to demonstrate Johnson's continuing concern over the relation of exceptionalism to whiteness. In making examples of Dunbar and Shiny, Johnson seeks to solidify his and his narrator's authentic black subject positions not in terms of the folk but at the more extreme level of genetics!

29  Again, I wish to emphasize that this is not my view, but one with which the narrator himself must wrestle. Throughout the course of his life, he equates white maleness with elevated class standings. This cultural construction of "authentic" whiteness is of particular importance because it represents one aspect of identity the narrator would like to retain even while writing himself more deeply into the folk-privileging discourse of blackness; it is this treacherous connection between class and race that he continually attempts to negotiate via his various racial performances.

30  Julian Mason, "James Weldon Johnson," 165.

31  I borrow the term "cultural mulatto" from Trey Ellis's essay "The New Black Aesthetic," *Callaloo* 12, no. 1 (winter 1989): 233.

32  Mencke, *Mulattoes and Race Mixture*, 170 (emphasis in original).

33  Bell, *Afro-American Novel*, 89.

34  Bell, *Afro-American Novel*, 88.

35  It should also be noted that Johnson lifts this passage verbatim and places it in his preface to *American Negro Poetry;* there is more than one instance of this sort of textual transfer between *Ex-Colored Man* and the preface. While there is some

distance between the consciousnesses of the narrator and Johnson himself, they also intersect quite neatly at particular junctures.

36 The question of minstrelsy as it relates to racial authenticity also appears explicitly in both Larsen and Schuyler. Not only is this a testament to the power of minstrelsy in defining, as Lott astutely argues, a baseline of American culture, but in the contexts of these African American writers, I think it also serves to further complicate the boundaries of black/white racial identity by pointing toward the ways in which ideas of "race" maintain specifically codified norms of performance. The question for these writers becomes the politics and aesthetics of these norms of performance and how the "less authentic" or liminal African American subject embraces or refuses them.

37 Eric Lott, *Love and Theft: Blackface Minstrelsy and the American Working Class* (New York: Oxford University Press, 1993), 39–40.

38 Nathan I. Huggins, *Harlem Renaissance* (New York: Oxford University Press, 1971), 152.

39 Lott, *Love and Theft*, 17.

40 There is much more that could be said here about minstrelsy and its complexities. I refer the interested reader to Lott as well as to Houston Baker's *Modernism and the Harlem Renaissance*, in which he takes up the question of minstrel masks, the politics of representation, and the performative in the context of his delineation of the concepts "the mastery of form" and "the deformation of mastery."

41 Dickson D. Bruce, "The South in African American Poetry, 1877–1915," *CLA Journal* 31 (September 1987): 23.

42 Huggins, *Harlem Renaissance*, 153.

43 Levy, *James Weldon Johnson*, 93.

44 Julian Mason, "James Weldon Johnson," 154.

45 Julian Mason, "James Weldon Johnson," 155.

46 Bronz, *Roots of Negro Racial Consciousness*, 30.

47 Huggins, *Harlem Renaissance*, 145.

48 It is important to note the narrator's decision to "let the world take [him] for what it would" (499), rather than to proclaim of his own accord his (false) whiteness. The narrator's passing is a passive act as much as a diligently pursued choice. Because he does not conform to certain class and geographic expectations, people "naturally" discount his blackness.

49 Berzon, *Neither White nor Black*, 159.

50 Huggins, *Harlem Renaissance*, 144.

51 Levy, *James Weldon Johnson*, 141.

52 Hall, "What Is This 'Black,'" 30.

### 3 *"Colored; cold. Wrong somewhere.": Jean Toomer's* Cane

1 Stuart Hall, "What Is This 'Black' in Black Popular Culture?" in *Black Popular Culture,* ed. Gina Dent (Seattle: Bay Press, 1992), 30.

2 Houston Baker employs this Satchmo quotation in his chapters on Toomer in *Singers at Daybreak* and *Afro-American Poetics* (the latter a revision of the former), although he does so in an effort to lay bare that "unknowable," intuitive space Armstrong had created rather than to reinforce it.

3 Hall, "What Is This 'Black,'" 28–29.

4 Henry Louis Gates Jr., *Figures in Black* (Oxford: Oxford University Press, 1987), 210.

5 Cynthia Earl Kerman and Richard Eldridge, *The Lives of Jean Toomer: A Hunger for Wholeness* (Baton Rouge: Louisiana State University Press, 1987), 80.

6 Jean Toomer, quoted in Darwin T. Turner, ed., *The Wayward and the Seeking* (Washington, D.C.: Howard University Press, 1980), 121.

7 Toomer, in Turner, *Wayward,* 133.

8 Jean Toomer to Claude McKay, quoted in Turner, *Wayward,* 18.

9 Jean Toomer, "The Blue Meridian," in Turner, *Wayward,* 217. Hereafter cited in the text.

10 Toomer, in Turner, *Wayward,* 85.

11 Toomer, in Turner, *Wayward,* 86.

12 Toomer's particular formulation of the issue at this point also has important resonances in contemporary critical theory. I am most struck with the way Toomer's statement meshes with Judith Butler's assertion in *Bodies That Matter* (New York: Routledge, 1993) that "the pluralist theoretical separation of [gender, race, ethnicity, and sexuality identifications] as 'categories' or indeed as 'positions' is itself based on exclusionary operations that attribute false uniformity to them and that serve the regulatory aims of the liberal state" (116).

13 Charles T. Davis, "Jean Toomer and the South: Region and Race as Elements within a Literary Imagination," *Studies in the Literary Imagination* 7 (fall 1974): 31.

14 Davis, "Jean Toomer and the South," 31.

15 Cary D. Wintz, *Black Culture and the Harlem Renaissance* (Houston: Rice University Press, 1988), 6. Wintz also goes on in his discussion of *Cane* to state that "exposure to the South triggered a passionate interest in [Toomer's] black heritage" (78). Wintz suggests an almost mystical link between geography and interest in racial identity, as if they were part and parcel of the same thing. I'm sure this comes as a surprise to many northern African Americans.

16 Kerman and Eldridge, *Lives of Jean Toomer,* 83.

17 Bernard Bell, *The Afro-American Novel and Its Tradition* (Amherst: University of Massachusetts Press, 1987), 99.

18 Toomer, in Turner, *Wayward*, 18.

19 Alice Walker, *In Search of Our Mothers' Gardens* (New York: Harcourt Brace, 1983), 64 (my emphasis).

20 Even in contemporary African American literature, one finds this kind of geographical comparison revisited. For instance, Trey Ellis contrasts African Americans in suburbia (or "upscale" neighborhoods) with those of the inner city in both *Platitudes* (1988) and *Home Repairs* (1993). Paul Beatty's *The White Boy Shuffle* (1996) similarly explores the differences setting can make by having the protagonist migrate from Santa Monica to South Central Los Angeles to collegiate Boston.

21 Nellie McKay, *Jean Toomer: Artist* (Chapel Hill: University of North Carolina Press, 1984), 89.

22 Jean Toomer, *Cane* (1923; New York: Liveright, 1975), 12. Hereafter cited in the text.

23 Toomer, in Turner, *Wayward*, 129.

24 Toomer, quoted in Turner, *Wayward*, 123.

25 I contend that this form of adopting an "alien," outside narrative voice to examine some notion of the racial "other" marks a significant achievement in the understanding of "race" as a social construction. This form of voice marks a break from naturalistic ideas of identity in that it allows the other to play the roles of both observed other and normative observer simultaneously. In doing so, the naturalized distinction between the two is shattered but appears to be discursively maintained. Charles Chesnutt's *The Conjure Woman* is a fine example of the ways narrative voice can be controlled quietly and thoroughly to shatter notions of racial difference.

26 Hall, "What Is This 'Black,'" 29.

27 Ladell Payne, *Black Novelists and the Southern Literary Tradition* (Athens: University of Georgia Press, 1981), 43.

28 McKay, *Jean Toomer: Artist*, 126.

29 McKay, *Jean Toomer: Artist*, 128.

30 John M. Reilly, "The Search for Black Redemption: Jean Toomer's *Cane*," *Studies in the Novel* 23 (fall 1970): 318. See also Robert H. Brinkmeyer Jr., "Wasted Talent, Wasted Art: The Literary Career of Jean Toomer," *Southern Quarterly* 20 (1981–1982), and McKay, *Jean Toomer: Artist*, for similar thoughts on section 2 of *Cane*. In my opinion, this appears to be a critical consensus.

31 Of interest here is a definition of soul. Is it the "soul" that, as Brinkmeyer would suggest, lends one black identity? Or is it "soul" in a more generally humanistic sense of "connection with humanity"? Although Toomer does not use the term himself, I suggest that the latter definition is more appropriate, given his dislike of racial labels and his predilection for a universalizing mysticism.

32 Brinkmeyer, "Wasted Talent," 80.

33 Again Toomer genders intraracial difference. His choice of metaphor is telling; its dehumanizing language demonstrates class prejudice combined with misogyny on John's part. On a deeper level, I think the language reveals a fundamental doubt on Toomer's part about the possibility of ever establishing solidarity based on traditional notions of "race." For him, the gulf between people lies on planes other than the black-white one.

34 Kerman and Eldridge, *Lives of Jean Toomer,* 345.

35 Walker, *Our Mothers' Gardens,* 63.

36 Tzvetan Todorov, " 'Race,' Writing, and Culture," in *"Race," Writing, and Difference,* ed. Henry Louis Gates Jr. (Chicago: University of Chicago Press, 1986), 370.

37 Quoted in Alan Golding, "Jean Toomer's *Cane:* The search for Identity through Form," *Arizona Quarterly* 39 (fall 1983): 211.

38 See McKay's chapter "The Circle of Experience: *Cane* (3)" for a particularly thorough treatment of "Kabnis."

39 McKay, *Jean Toomer: Artist,* 151.

40 Butler, *Bodies That Matter,* 95.

41 This is also a significant gendering of geography. Kabnis, in a sense, returns to the womb, to his place of origin, the place from which his ancestors, "the Southern blue-bloods" (107), came. He learns that one cannot return to the womb, yet Toomer continues to represent the South as the birth giver to blackness.

42 Butler, *Bodies That Matter,* 115.

### 4 *A Clash of Birthrights: Nella Larsen, the Feminine, and African American Identity*

1 Hazel Carby's *Reconstructing Womanhood* (New York: Oxford University Press, 1987) explores at great length "the cult of true womanhood" and its discourse. I am very much indebted to Carby's ideas, particularly those in the first two chapters of her book.

2 Judith Butler, *Bodies That Matter* (New York: Routledge, 1993), 116.

3 Langston Hughes, "Cross," in *Selected Poems* (1959; New York: Vintage, 1974), 158.

4 Deborah McDowell, introduction to *"Quicksand" and "Passing,"* by Nella Larsen (1928–1929; New Brunswick: Rutgers University Press, 1986), xvii.

5 The irony of such a position is that it reinforces the legal fictions of "race" perpetuated under slavery; that is, the child "follows the condition of the mother." Rather than being a liberating position—which is perhaps not Hughes's intent at all—the location of blackness as originating in the feminine reproduces both racial and gender hierarchies and their interrelatedness.

6 John Mencke, *Mulattoes and Race Mixture* (Ann Arbor: UMI Press, 1979), 144.

7  I should also like to point out that George Schuyler, as we shall see in the next chapter, also ends up engaging Langston Hughes in a debate about black authenticity. Hailed for his pioneering and invaluable work with a jazz aesthetic and other forms of African American folk culture, Hughes also becomes the focus of critique by Harlem Renaissance contemporaries more ambivalent than he about folk-based African American authenticity.

8  Ann E. Hostetler, "The Aesthetics of Race and Gender in Nella Larsen's *Quicksand*," *PMLA* 105 (1990): 35.

9  Nella Larsen, *"Quicksand" and "Passing"* (1928–1929; New Brunswick: Rutgers University Press, 1986), 5. Hereafter cited in the text.

10  Hazel Carby, *Reconstructing Womanhood* (New York: Oxford University Press, 1987), 171 (my emphasis). Further, Bernard Bell and Judith Berzon, among others, have noted this dual discomfort with folk and bourgeoisie in *Quicksand*.

11  Lillie P. Howard, "A Lack Somewhere: Nella Larsen's *Quicksand*," in *The Harlem Renaissance Re-examined,* ed. Victor Kramer (New York: AMS Press, 1987), 226.

12  Hostetler, "Aesthetics," 39.

13  What remains largely unspoken, untheorized, and unquestioned both in this study and more generally is this complex relationship between individual and racial identity. Are these concepts perhaps philosophically opposed to each other? Does an insistence on the individual ignore the power of social categories and social relations in problematic ways? Does privileging the group-dependent notion of "race" oversimplify the multiple, and often contestatory, identifications of the individual subject?

14  Hostetler, "Aesthetics," 38.

15  Carby, *Reconstructing Womanhood,* 175.

16  Paula Giddings, *When and Where I Enter* (New York: William Morrow, 1984), 192.

17  Cheryl A. Wall, "Passing for What? Aspects of Identity in Nella Larsen's Novels," *Black American Literature Forum* 20 (1986): 98.

18  Priscilla Ramsey, "Freeze the Day: A Feminist Reading of *Quicksand* and *Passing*," *Afro-Americans in New York Life and History* 9 (January 1985): 38.

19  Ramsey, "Freeze the Day," 31.

20  Carby, *Reconstructing Womanhood,* 174.

21  Michelle Wallace, "Variation on Negation," in *Reading Black, Reading Feminist,* ed. Henry Louis Gates Jr. (New York: Meridian, 1990), 58.

22  See Carby, *Reconstructing Womanhood,* particularly the second chapter, "Slave and Mistress."

23  Hortense Spillers, "Mama's Baby, Papa's Maybe: An American Grammar Book," *Diacritics* (summer 1987): 80 (emphasis in original).

24  Mary Helen Washington, "The Darkened Eye Restored: Notes toward a Literary History of Black Women," in Gates, *Reading Black,* 37.

25  Wall, "Passing for What?" 99.

26  Carby, *Reconstructing Womanhood*, 174.

27  Carby, *Reconstructing Womanhood*, 27.

28  E. Franklin Frazier, *Black Bourgeoisie* (New York: Free Press, 1957), 195.

29  Giddings, *When and Where I Enter*, 191.

30  On the train north, Helga thinks about her relationship with James in the following way: "Acute nausea rose in her as she recalled the slight quivering of his lips sometimes when her hands unexpectedly touched his" (24). Given Larsen's penchant for irony, I would not call this a passage of sexual repression; rather, it is more an expression of relief from a distasteful lover.

31  Carby, *Reconstructing Womanhood*, 27.

32  Wall, "Passing for What?" 100.

33  Wall, "Passing for What?" 100.

34  Although Larsen implies that Helga's frustration with "race" talk is not well thought out, she also adds this sentiment at the end of a brutal attack on the hypocritical and ineffectual nature of the uplifters' "race consciousness." Whereas Helga may be acting from emotion as much as reason, we are not led to believe that her position is absolutely devoid of merit.

35  McDowell, introduction, xix.

36  Wall, "Passing for What?" 103.

37  Jean Toomer, *Cane* (1923; New York: Liveright, 1975), 77.

38  Butler, *Bodies That Matter*, 117.

39  Hostetler, "Aesthetics," 43.

40  Reminiscent of the conversion scenes of Langston Hughes's *The Big Sea* or James Baldwin's *Go Tell It on the Mountain*, Larsen uses this chapter of the novel to problematize entrée into a community toward which she has had—throughout the text—ambivalent feelings at best.

41  Hostetler, "Aesthetics," 44.


5  *Color, Culture, and the Nature of Race: George S. Schuyler's*
Black No More

1  Henry Louis Gates Jr., "A Fragmented Man: George Schuyler and the Claims of Race," *New York Times Book Review*, 20 September 1992, 42.

2  Gates, "Fragmented," 42.

3  Gino Speranza, *Race or Nation* (Indianapolis: Bobbs-Merrill, 1925), 25.

4  Speranza, *Race or Nation*, 266.

5  George S. Schuyler, *Black and Conservative* (New Rochelle, N.Y.: Arlington House, 1966), 157.

6  I refer to the character in this manner because I wish to emphasize the arbitrary nature between signifier and signified that Schuyler brings forth in this text.

When Max transforms himself into Matt, only the signifier changes, not the man signified by it; similarly, the signifiers of race change via Crookman's process, but it is the failure of a system based on the essential connection between signifier and signified that plunges the world of the novel into chaos.

7  George S. Schuyler, *Black No More: Being an Account of the Strange and Wonderful Workings of Science in the Land of the Free, A.D. 1933–1940* (1931; Boston: Northeastern University Press, 1989), 40. Hereafter cited in the text.

8  Harry M. Williams Jr., "When Black Is Right: The Life and Writings of George S. Schuyler" (Ph.D. diss., Brown University, 1988), 15.

9  Williams, "When Black Is Right," 20.

10  George S. Schuyler, "Our White Folks," *American Mercury* 12, no. 48 (December 1927): 390.

11  Here it might be productive to revisit one of Alice Walker's criticisms of Jean Toomer, namely, that "an absence of black people assured the absence of racism." What fascinates me is that this position is *literalized* in *Black No More* in a way that Toomer never imagined. It is through the production of physical whiteness in Schuyler's novel that the possible merit of Toomer's critique of discursive racial categories becomes clearer. The problem is not color itself but the social stigma or privilege that color carries with it.

12  It is interesting to note, however, that Schuyler's solution of miscegenation as the answer to the "race problem" (see "A Negro Looks Ahead," *American Mercury* 21 [February 1930]: 469–76) ultimately approximates Crookman's plan more closely than Beard's. The major difference in Schuyler's vision, though, is that both "black" and "white" would be eliminated as defining categories, whereas for Crookman, "white" remains the defining category at the expense of "black." Tellingly, it is Schuyler's vision that becomes actualized at the end of *Black No More*.

13  Schuyler, *Black and Conservative*, 157.

14  George S. Schuyler, "The Negro-Art Hokum," *The Nation* 121, no. 3180 (16 June 1926): 662.

15  Schuyler, "Hokum," 662.

16  Schuyler, "Hokum," 663.

17  Langston Hughes, "The Negro Artist and the Racial Mountain," *The Nation* 122, no. 3181 (23 June 1926): 693.

18  Schuyler, "Hokum," 662.

19  Hughes, "Negro Artist," 692. One might also want to consider the paradox of Hughes's own language here: What is "racial individuality"? Is it the characteristic of an entire class of people, or isn't it? What does it mean to attribute a common individuality to millions of people? For me, this is a potential oxymoron that one finds at the very heart of much of American literature, whether written by blacks or whites. This notion finds its analogue in popular culture in

the old soft-drink commercial that asks us to be part of the "original crowd" by consuming the product; the safest sort of individuation derives from adopting a collective, coherent identity.

20  Schuyler, *Black and Conservative,* 137.

21  For Schuyler's distaste for cosmetic skin lightening, see "Our White Folks," *Black No More* and its parody of Madam C. J. Walker (Sisseretta Blandish), and his later piece "Do Negroes Want to Be White?" *American Mercury* 182 (June 1956): 55–60.

22  Schuyler, "Our White Folks," 392.

23  Schuyler, "Our White Folks," 392.

24  Schuyler, "Our White Folks," 387.

25  Hughes, "Negro Artist," 692.

26  Hughes, "Negro Artist," 694.

27  Williams, "When Black Is Right," 183.

28  Walter White, "The Paradox of Color," in *The New Negro,* ed. Alain Locke (1925; Atheneum: New York, 1968), 366.

29  Williams, "When Black Is Right," 187.

30  Some linguists have, indeed, drawn a correlation between race and dialect; of particular note, I find Shirley Brice Heath's informative ethnography *Ways with Words* (Cambridge: Cambridge University Press, 1983). And although Heath would challenge Crookman's assertion about the primacy of sectional dialects, she also writes: "In this geographic region . . . socioeconomic differences among children seemed useless as a variable against which to set their language differences. Ascribing Black, Southern, or Standard English to speakers by racial membership was also not satisfactory to these students, for almost all of them, black and white, could shift varieties as occasion demanded. . . . They had an endless store of anecdotes about children *learning* to use across and within groups of the region" (3, my emphasis). What I find particularly important in this passage is the insistence on language as a performative and learned marker of identity, rather than an innate race, class, or geographic trait.

31  George S. Schuyler, "The Caucasian Problem," in *What the Negro Wants,* ed. Rayford W. Logan (Chapel Hill: University of North Carolina Press, 1944), 284.

32  Schuyler, "A Negro Looks Ahead," 213.

33  This formulation of the problem is echoed years later in Paul Gilroy's study *"There Ain't No Black in the Union Jack": The Cultural Politics of Race and Nation* (Chicago: University of Chicago Press, 1987). Of particular interest is chapter 1, " 'Race,' Class, and Agency," in which Gilroy offers a suggestive reading of the intricate relations between "race" and class in Britain.

34  I also wish to note that Schuyler makes clear the real possibility of being both black *and* bourgeois as a viable subject position. Max/Matt's blackness is never questioned; it is merely superficially erased. Nor does Schuyler critique him for

"bourgeois pretensions" outside the realm of possible black identity (in a way E. Franklin Frazier might). In fact, Schuyler solidifies Max/Matt's subject position by contrasting it with white bourgeois pretension. Recall Max/Matt's wife, and Givens's daughter, Helen, whose "'finishing school' about finished what intelligence [she] possessed" while allowing her "enough superficialities to enable her to get by in the 'best' circles of society and a great deal of that shallow facetiousness that passes for sophistication in American upper-class life" (74).

35 Hazel Carby, *Reconstructing Womanhood* (New York: Oxford University Press, 1987), 25.

36 Max/Matt is not the only African American male in the text who views whiteness with sexual desire. Schuyler sets up Crookman as a (mocking) example of a "race man," remarking, "He was wedded to everything black except a black woman—his wife was a white girl with remote Negro ancestry" (55). I mention this to emphasize that difference and desire are always linked in *Black No More;* Mr. and Mrs. Givens, a same-race couple, are alternately represented as asexual or desireless.

37 Joel Williamson, *New People* (New York: Free Press, 1980), 199–200.

38 Gunnar Myrdal, *An American Dilemma* (New York: Harper, 1944), 125, 134.

39 James Hugo Johnston, *Race Relations in Virginia and Miscegenation in the South* (Amherst: University of Massachusetts Press, 1970), 215.

40 Schuyler, "A Negro Looks Ahead," 220.

41 Schuyler, "The Caucasian Problem," 285.

42 Michael W. Peplow, *George S. Schuyler* (Boston: Twayne, 1980), 77–78.

43 Schuyler, "The Caucasian Problem," 298.

44 Ann Rayson, "George Schuyler: Paradox among 'Assimilationist Writers,'" *Black American Literature Forum* (fall 1978): 106.

45 Williams, "When Black Is Right," 188.


6 *The Possibilities of Multiplicity: Community, Tradition, and African American Subject Positions*

1 J. Hillis Miller, *Tropes, Parables, Performatives* (Durham: Duke University Press, 1991), ix.

2 M. H. Abrams, *A Glossary of Literary Terms* (New York: Holt Rinehart and Winston, 1981), 63.

3 Judith Butler, *Gender Trouble: Feminism and the Subversion of Identity* (New York: Routledge, 1989), 140.

4 Trey Ellis, "The New Black Aesthetic," *Callaloo* 12, no. 1 (winter 1989): 235.

5 bell hooks, "Marginality as a Site of Resistance," in *Out There: Marginalization and Contemporary Cultures,* ed. Russell Ferguson et al. (New York: Museum of Contemporary Art, 1990), 341.

6  hooks, 342.

7  hooks, 341; Ellis, "The New Black Aesthetic," 235.

8  Theodore G. Vincent, ed., *Voices of a Black Nation: Political Journalism in the Harlem Renaissance* (San Francisco: Ramparts Press, 1973), 28.

9  Henry Louis Gates Jr., "The Blackness of Blackness: A Critique of the Sign and the Signifying Monkey," in *Black Literature and Literary Theory*, ed. Henry Louis Gates Jr. (New York: Methuen, 1984), 286.

10  Linda Hutcheon, *The Politics of Postmodernism* (New York: Routledge, 1989), 1.

11  Trey Ellis, *Platitudes* (New York: Vintage, 1988), 67. Hereafter cited in the text.

12  Henry Louis Gates Jr., "Writing 'Race' and the Difference It Makes," in *"Race," Writing, and Difference* (Chicago: University of Chicago Press, 1986), 11.

13  Benedict Anderson, *Imagined Communities: Reflections on the Origin and Spread of Nationalism* (London: Verso, 1983), 15.

14  Anderson, *Imagined Communities*, 16.

15  Kwame Anthony Appiah, "The Conservation of 'Race,'" *Black American Literature Forum* 32, no. 1 (spring 1989): 52.

16  Cornel West, "The New Cultural Politics of Difference," in Ferguson, *Out There*, 29.

17  Frantz Fanon, *The Wretched of the Earth* (1961; New York: Grove Press, 1968), 223.

18  Albert C. Barnes, "Negro Art and America," in *The New Negro*, ed. Alain Locke (1925; New York: Atheneum, 1968), 24–25.

19  Ellis, "The New Black Aesthetic," 251.

20  Appiah, "Conservation," 55.

21  West, "New Cultural Politics," 29.

22  Eric Hobsbawm, "Introduction: Inventing Traditions," in *The Invention of Tradition*, ed. Eric Hobsbawm and Terrance Ranger (Cambridge: Cambridge University Press, 1983), 12.

23  Kwame Anthony Appiah, "Out of Africa: Topologies of Nativism," in *The Bounds of Race: Perspectives on Hegemony and Resistance*, ed. Dominick LaCapra (Ithaca: Cornell University Press, 1991), 150.

24  West, "New Cultural Politics," 33; Ellis, "The New Black Aesthetic," 239.

25  Hobsbawm, "Inventing Traditions," 2.

26  Butler, *Gender Trouble*, 145.

27  Stuart Hall, "New Ethnicities," in *"Race," Culture, and Difference*, ed. James Donald and Ali Rattansi (London: Sage Publications, 1992), 254–55.

28  It might prove fruitful to think of the ongoing debate over the literary canon as a variation of this sort of reimagining. In some ways, it is a clash over two different visions of community and the invented traditions that help "legitimize" or "authenticate" these communities' sense of identity. Further, a broader, more inclusive canon would not necessarily end the debate (and neither would a nar-

rower one); we must anticipate an eventual reimagination of that community
and its invented tradition as well. The process is dynamic rather than static.

29  West, "New Cultural Politics," 35.

30  Patrick Joyce, *Visions of the People* (Cambridge: Cambridge University Press, 1991), 330.

31  Ellis, "The New Black Aesthetic," 238.

32  John Henrik Clarke, "The Reclaiming of African History," in *African Culture,* ed. Molife Kente Asante and Kariamu Welsh Asante (1985; Trenton: First Africa World Press, 1990), 163.

33  Ellis, "The New Black Aesthetic," 251.

# Bibliography

Abrams, M. H. *A Glossary of Literary Terms.* New York: Holt, Rinehart and Winston, 1981.

Anderson, Benedict. *Imagined Communities: Reflections on the Origin and Spread of Nationalism.* London: Verso, 1983.

Appiah, Kwame Anthony. "The Conservation of 'Race.'" *Black American Literature Forum* 32, no. 1 (spring 1989): 37–60.

———. "Out of Africa: Topologies of Nativism." In LaCapra, *The Bounds of Race,* 134–63.

Asante, Molife K. *The Afrocentric Idea.* Philadelphia: Temple University Press, 1987.

Asante, Molife, and Kariamu Welsh Asante, eds. *African Culture.* 1985. Trenton: First World Press, 1990.

Baker, Houston A., Jr. *Afro-American Poetics: Revisions of Harlem and the Black Aesthetic.* Madison: University of Wisconsin Press, 1988.

———. *Blues Ideology and Afro-American Literature: A Vernacular Theory.* Chicago: University of Chicago Press, 1984.

———. *The Journey Back.* Chicago: University of Chicago Press, 1980.

———. *Modernism and the Harlem Renaissance.* Chicago: University of Chicago Press, 1987.

———. *Singers at Daybreak.* Washington, D.C.: Howard University Press, 1983.

Baker, Houston A., Jr., and Patricia Redmond, eds. *Afro-American Literary Study in the 1990's.* Chicago: University of Chicago Press, 1989.

Baldwin, James. *Go Tell It on the Mountain.* 1952. New York: Dell, 1985.

Balibar, Etienne. "Paradoxes of Universality." Trans. Michael Edwards. In Goldberg, *Anatomy of Racism,* 283–94.

Barnes, Albert C. "Negro Art and America." In Locke, *The New Negro,* 19–28.

Beemyn, Brett. "A Bibliography of Works by and about Nella Larsen." *African American Review* 26, no. 1 (spring 1992): 183–88.

Bell, Bernard W. *The Afro-American Novel and Its Traditions.* Amherst: University of Massachusetts Press, 1987.

Berzon, Judith R. *Neither White nor Black.* New York: New York University Press, 1978.

*Black Is . . . Black Ain't.* Dir. Marlon T. Riggs. Independent Television Series, 1995.

Bone, Robert A. *Down Home.* New York: Capricorn Books, 1975.

Bontemps, Arna, ed. *The Harlem Renaissance Remembered.* New York: Dodd, 1972.

Bordo, Susan. "Feminism, Postmodernism, and Gender-Skepticism." In Nicholson, *Feminism/Postmodernism*, 133–56.

Brinkmeyer, Robert H., Jr. "Wasted Talent, Wasted Art: The Literary Career of Jean Toomer." *Southern Quarterly* 20 (1981–1982): 7584.

Bronz, Stephen H. *Roots of Negro Racial Consciousness.* New York: Libra, 1964.

Bruce, Dickson D. "The South in African American Poetry, 1877–1915." *CLA Journal* 31 (September 1987): 12–30.

Butler, Judith. *Bodies That Matter: On the Discursive Limits of "Sex."* New York: Routledge, 1993.

———. *Gender Trouble: Feminism and the Subversion of Identity.* New York: Routledge, 1989.

———. "Gender Trouble, Feminist Theory, and Psychoanalytic Discourse." In Nicholson, *Feminism/Postmodernism*, 324–40.

Byrd, Rudolph P. "Jean Toomer and the Afro-American Literary Tradition." *Callaloo* 8, no. 2 (spring–summer 1985): 310–19.

Caldiera, Maria Isabel. "Jean Toomer's *Cane:* The Anxiety of the Modern Artist." *Callaloo* 8, no. 3 (fall 1985): 544–50.

Carby, Hazel V. "Ideologies of Black Folk: The Historical Novel of Slavery." In McDowell and Rampersad, *Slavery and the Literary Imagination*, 104–24.

———. *Reconstructing Womanhood.* New York: Oxford University Press, 1987.

Chace, Patricia. "The Women in *Cane.*" *CLA Journal* 14 (March 1971): 259–73.

Chesnutt, Charles. *The Conjure Woman.* 1899. Ann Arbor: University of Michigan Press, 1969.

———. *The Marrow of Tradition.* 1901. Ann Arbor: University of Michigan Press, 1969.

Clarke, John Henrik. "The Reclaiming of African History." In Asante and Asante, *African Culture*, 157–72.

Cross, William E. *Shades of Black: Diversity in African-American Identity.* Philadelphia: Temple University Press, 1991.

Cruse, Harold. *The Crisis of the Negro Intellectual.* 1967. New York: Quill, 1984.

Davis, Arthur P. *From the Dark Tower.* Washington, D.C.: Howard University Press, 1974.

Davis, Charles T. "Jean Toomer and the South: Region and Race as Elements within a Literary Imagination." *Studies in the Literary Imagination* 7 (fall 1974): 25–37.

Davis, F. James. *Who Is Black?* University Park: Pennsylvania State University Press, 1991.

Dent, Gina, ed. *Black Popular Culture.* Seattle: Bay Press, 1992.

Donald, James, and Ali Rattansi, eds. *"Race," Culture, and Difference.* London: Sage Publications, 1992.

Douglass, Frederick. *Narrative of the Life of Frederick Douglass, an American Slave, Written by Himself.* New York: Viking, 1982.

DuBois, W. E. B. "Criteria of Negro Art." *Crisis* 32 (October 1926): 296–98.

———. *The Souls of Black Folk.* 1903. New York: Signet, 1968.

———. "A Younger Literary Movement." *Crisis* 27 (February 1924): 161–63.

Durham, Frank. "Jean Toomer's Vision of the Southern Negro." *Southern Humanities Review* 6 (winter 1972): 13–22.

Ellis, Trey. "The New Black Aesthetic." *Callaloo* 21, no. 1 (winter 1989): 233–43.

———. *Platitudes.* New York: Vintage, 1988.

———. "Response to NBA Critiques." *Callaloo* 21, no. 1 (winter 1989): 250–51.

Fanon, Frantz. *The Wretched of the Earth.* 1961. New York: Grove Press, 1968.

Faulkner, Howard. "James Weldon Johnson's Portrait of the Artist as Invisible Man." *Black American Literature Forum* 19, no. 4 (winter 1985): 147–51.

Ferguson, Russell, ed. *Out There: Marginalization and Contemporary Cultures.* New York: Museum of Contemporary Art, 1990.

Flemming, Robert E. *James Weldon Johnson and Arna Wendell Bontemps: A Reference Guide.* Boston: G. K. Hall, 1978.

Forgacs, David, ed. *An Antonio Gramsci Reader.* New York: Schocken, 1988.

Foucault, Michel. *The Archaeology of Knowledge.* Trans. A. M. Sheridan Smith. New York: Harper and Row, 1972.

Franklin, John Hope, ed. *Three Negro Classics.* New York: Avon, 1965.

Frazier, E. Franklin. *Black Bourgeoisie.* New York: Free Press, 1957.

French, Warren, ed. *The Twenties: Fiction, Poetry, and Drama.* DeLand, Fla.: Everett/Edwards, 1975.

Fullwinder, S. P. "Jean Toomer: Lost Generation, or Negro Renaissance?" *Phylon* 27 (1966): 396–403.

Gallagher, Brian. "Explorations of Black Identity from *The New Negro* to *Invisible Man.*" *Perspectives on Contemporary Literature* 8 (1983): 1–9.

Gates, Henry Louis, Jr. "Canon Formation, Literary History, and the Afro-American Tradition: From the Seen to the Told." In Baker and Redmond, *Afro-American Literary Study,* 14–38.

———. *Figures in Black: Words, Signs, and the "Racial" Self.* New York: Oxford University Press, 1987.

———. "A Fragmented Man: George S. Schuyler and the Claims of Race." *New York Times Book Review,* 20 September 1992, 42.

————. "Writing 'Race' and the Difference It Makes." In Gates, *"Race," Writing, and Difference*, 1–20.

————, ed. *Black Literature and Literary Theory*. New York: Methuen, 1984.

————, ed. "The Black Person in Art: How Should S/He Be Portrayed?" *Black American Literature Forum* 21, nos. 1–2 (spring–summer 1987): 3–24.

————, ed. "The Black Person in Art: How Should S/He Be Portrayed? (Part 2)." *Black American Literature Forum* 21, no. 3 (fall 1987): 317–32.

————, ed. *"Race," Writing, and Difference*. Chicago: University of Chicago Press, 1986.

————, ed. *Reading Black, Reading Feminist*. New York: Meridian, 1990.

Giddings, Paula. *When and Where I Enter*. New York: William Morrow, 1984.

Gilroy, Paul. *There Ain't No Black in the Union Jack: The Cultural Politics of Race and Nation*. 1987. Chicago: University of Chicago Press, 1991.

Goldberg, David Theo, ed. *Anatomy of Racism*. Minneapolis: University of Minnesota Press, 1990.

Golding, Alan. "Jean Toomer's *Cane:* The Search for Identity through Form." *Arizona Quarterly* 39 (fall 1983): 197–214.

Gruesser, John C. "Afro-American Travel Literature and Africanist Discourse." *Black American Literature Forum* 24, no. 1 (spring 1990): 5–20.

Hall, Stuart. "New Ethnicities." In Donald and Rattansi, *"Race," Culture, and Difference*, 252–59.

————. "What Is This 'Black' in Black Popular Culture?" In Dent, *Black Popular Culture*, 21–33.

Haller, Mark H. *Eugenics: Hereditarian Attitudes in American Thought*. New Brunswick: Rutgers University Press, 1963.

Harding, Sandra, and Jean O'Barr, eds. *Sex and Scientific Inquiry*. Chicago: University of Chicago Press, 1987.

Heath, Shirley Brice. *Ways with Words*. Cambridge: Cambridge University Press, 1983.

Hobsbawm, Eric, and Terrance Ranger, eds. *The Invention of Tradition*. Cambridge: Cambridge University Press, 1983.

Hodge, John L. "Equality: Beyond Dualism and Oppression." In Goldberg, *Anatomy of Racism*, 89–107.

Holt, Thomas C. "The Political Uses of Alienation: W. E. B. DuBois on Politics, Race, and Culture, 1903–1940." *American Quarterly* 42, no. 2 (June 1990): 301–23.

hooks, bell. *Black Looks: Race and Representation*. Boston: South End Press, 1992.

————. "Marginality as a Site of Resistance." In Ferguson, *Out There*, 341–43.

————. "Talking Back." In Ferguson, *Out There*, 337–40.

Hostetler, Ann E. "The Aesthetics of Race and Gender in Nella Larsen's *Quicksand*." *PMLA* 105, no. 1 (1990): 35–46.

Howard, Lillie P. "A Lack Somewhere: Nella Larsen's *Quicksand*." In Kramer, *The Harlem Renaissance Re-examined*, 210–30.

Huggins, Nathan I. *Harlem Renaissance*. New York: Oxford University Press, 1971.

Hughes, Langston. *The Big Sea*. 1940. New York: Thunder's Mouth Press, 1990.

———. "The Negro Artist and the Racial Mountain." *The Nation* 122 (23 June 1926): 692–94.

———. *Selected Poems*. 1959. New York: Vintage, 1974.

Hull, Gloria. *Color, Sex, and Poetry*. Bloomington: Indiana University Press, 1987.

Hurston, Zora Neale. *Their Eyes Were Watching God*. 1937. New York: Harper and Row, 1990.

Hutcheon, Linda. *The Politics of Postmodernism*. New York: Routledge, 1989.

Hutchinson, George B. "Jean Toomer and the 'New Negroes' of Washington." *American Literature* 63, no. 4 (December 1991): 683–92.

Jackson, Blyden. "The Harlem Renaissance." In Rubin, *Comic Imagination*, 295–303.

———. "Renaissance in the Twenties." In French, *The Twenties*, 303–16.

Johnson, James Weldon. *Along This Way*. New York: Viking, 1933.

———. *The Autobiography of an Ex-Colored Man*. In Franklin, *Three Negro Classics*, 390–511.

———, ed. *The Book of American Negro Poetry*. New York: Harcourt, Brace, 1922.

Johnston, James Hugo. *Race Relations in Virginia and Miscegenation in the South*. Amherst: University of Massachusetts Press, 1970.

Joyce, Patrick. *Visions of the People*. Cambridge: Cambridge University Press, 1991.

Kerman, Cynthia Earl, and Richard Eldridge. *The Lives of Jean Toomer: A Hunger for Wholeness*. Baton Rouge: Louisiana State University Press, 1987.

Kramer, Victor, ed. *The Harlem Renaissance Re-examined*. New York: AMS Press, 1987.

LaCapra, Dominic, ed. *The Bounds of Race: Perspectives on Hegemony and Resistance*. Ithaca: Cornell University Press, 1991.

Landry, Bart. *The New Black Middle Class*. Berkeley: University of California Press, 1987.

Larsen, Nella. *"Quicksand" and "Passing."* 1928. American Women Writers Series. New Brunswick: Rutgers University Press, 1986.

Lemann, Nicholas. *The Promised Land: The Great Black Migration and How It Changed America*. New York: Knopf, 1991.

Levy, Eugene. *James Weldon Johnson*. Chicago: University of Chicago Press, 1973.

Lewis, David Levering. *When Harlem Was in Vogue*. New York: Oxford University Press, 1979.

Little, Jonathan. "Nella Larsen's *Passing*: Irony and the Critics." *African American Review* 26, no. 1 (spring 1992): 173–82.

Locke, Alain. "Negro Youth Speaks." In Locke, *The New Negro*, 47–53.

———. "The New Negro." In Locke, *The New Negro*, 3–18.

————, ed. *The New Negro*. 1925. New York: Atheneum, 1968.

Logan, Rayford W. *What the Negro Wants*. Chapel Hill: University of North Carolina Press, 1944.

Lott, Eric. *Love and Theft: Blackface Minstrelsy and the American Working Class*. New York: Oxford University Press, 1993.

Lubiano, Wahneema. "Henry Louis Gates, Jr., and African-American Literary Discourse." *New England Quarterly* 62, no. 4 (1990): 561–72.

Madigan, Mark J. "Miscegenation and 'The Dicta of Race and Class': The Rhinelander Case and Nella Larsen's *Passing.*" *Modern Fiction Studies* 36, no. 4 (winter 1990): 523–29.

Mason, Julian. "James Weldon Johnson: A Southern Writer Resists the South." *CLA Journal* 31 (December 1987): 154–69.

Mason, Mary G. "Travel as Metaphor and Reality in Afro-American Women's Autobiography, 1850–1972." *Black American Literature Forum* 24, no. 2 (summer 1990): 337–56.

McDowell, Deborah. Introduction to Larsen, *"Quicksand" and "Passing,"* ix–xxxii.

McDowell, Deborah, and Arnold Rampersad, eds. *Slavery and the Literary Imagination*. Baltimore: Johns Hopkins University Press, 1989.

McKay, Nellie. *Jean Toomer: Artist*. Chapel Hill: University of North Carolina Press, 1984.

Mencke, John G. *Mulattoes and Race Mixture: American Attitudes and Images*. Ann Arbor: UMI Research Press, 1979.

Miller, J. Hillis. *Tropes, Parables, Performatives*. Durham: Duke University Press, 1991.

Moses, Wilson J. "The Lost World of the Negro, 1895–1919: Black Literary and Intellectual Life before the 'Renaissance.'" *Black American Literature Forum* 21, nos. 1–2 (spring–summer 1987): 61–84.

Munro, C. Lynn. "Jean Toomer: A Bibliography of Secondary Sources." *Black American Literature Forum* 21, no. 3 (fall 1987): 275–87.

Myrdal, Gunnar. *An American Dilemma*. New York: Harper, 1944.

Nicholson, Linda J., ed. *Feminism/Postmodernism*. New York: Routledge, 1990.

Outlaw, Lucius. "Toward a Critical Theory of 'Race.'" In Goldberg, *Anatomy of Racism*, 58–82.

Parham, Thomas A. "Cycles of Psychological Nigrescence." *The Counseling Psychologist* 17, no. 2 (April 1989): 187–225.

Payne, Ladell. *Black Novelists and the Southern Literary Tradition*. Athens: University of Georgia Press, 1981.

Peplow, Michael. "The Black 'Picaro' in Schuyler's *Black No More.*" *Crisis* (January 1976): 7–10.

————. *George S. Schuyler*. Boston: Twayne, 1980.

————. "George Schuyler, Satirist: Rhetorical Devices in *Black No More.*" *CLA Journal* (January 1976): 242–57.

Potter, Vilma R. "Race and Poetry: Two Anthologies of the Twenties." *CLA Journal* 29 (March 1986): 276–87.

Pryse, Marjorie, and Hortense Spillers, eds. *Conjuring: Black Women, Fiction, and Literary Tradition*. Bloomington: Indiana University Press, 1985.

Ramsey, Priscilla. "Freeze the Day: A Feminist Reading of *Quicksand* and *Passing*." *Afro-Americans in New York Life and History* 9 (January 1985): 27–41.

Rayson, Ann. "George S. Schuyler: Paradox among 'Assimilationist Writers.'" *Black American Literature Forum* (fall 1978): 102–6.

Reilly, John M. "The Black Anti-utopian." *Black American Literature Forum* (fall 1978): 107–9.

————. "The Search for Black Redemption: Jean Toomer's *Cane*." *Studies in the Novel* 23 (fall 1970): 312–29.

Reuter, Edward Byron. *The Mulatto in the United States*. Boston: Gorham, 1918.

Rubin, Louis D., ed. *The Comic Imagination in American Literature*. New Brunswick: Rutgers University Press, 1973.

Schomburg, Arthur. "The Negro Digs Up His Past." In Locke, *The New Negro*, 231–37.

Schuyler, George S. *Black and Conservative*. New Rochelle, N.Y.: Arlington House, 1966.

————. *Black No More: Being an Account of the Strange and Wonderful Workings of Science in the Land of the Free, A.D. 1933–1940*. 1933. Boston: Northeastern University Press, 1989.

————. "The Caucasian Problem." In Logan, *What the Negro Wants*, 280–305.

————. "Do Negroes Want to Be White?" *American Mercury* 182 (June 1956): 55–60.

————. "The Negro-Art Hokum." *The Nation* 121 (16 June 1926): 662–63.

————. "A Negro Looks Ahead." *American Mercury* 29 (February 1930): 212–20.

————. "Our White Folks." *American Mercury* 12 (December 1927): 385–92.

Singh, Amritjit. "Beyond the Mountain: Langston Hughes on Race/Class and Art." *Langston Hughes Review* 6, no. 1 (spring 1987): 37–43.

————, ed. *The Harlem Renaissance: Revaluations*. New York: Garland, 1989.

Smith, Valerie. "Black Feminist Theory." In Wall, *Changing Our Own Words*, 38–57.

Sollers, Werner. *Beyond Ethnicity*. New York: Oxford University Press, 1986.

Speranza, Gino. *Race or Nation*. Indianapolis: Bobbs-Merril, 1925.

Spillers, Hortense. "Mama's Baby, Papa's Maybe: An American Grammar Book." *Diacritics* (summer 1987): 65–81.

Thornton, Jerome E. "'Goin' on de Muck': The Paradoxical Journey of the Black American Hero." *CLA Journal* 31, no. 3 (March 1988): 261–80.

Thurman, Wallace. *The Blacker the Berry . . .* 1929. New York: Macmillan, 1970.

Todorov, Tzvetan. "'Race,' Writing, and Culture." In Gates, *"Race," Writing, and Difference*, 370–80.

Toomer, Jean. *Cane*. 1923. New York: Liveright, 1975.

Turner, Darwin T. *The Wayward and the Seeking.* Washington, D.C.: Howard University Press, 1980.

Vincent, Theodore G., ed. *Voices of a Black Nation: Political Journalism in the Harlem Renaissance.* San Francisco: Ramparts Press, 1973.

Waldron, Edward E. "The Search for Identity in Jean Toomer's 'Esther.'" *CLA Journal* 14, no. 3 (March 1971): 277–80.

Walker, Alice. *In Search of Our Mothers' Gardens.* New York: Harcourt Brace, 1983.

Wall, Cheryl. "Passing for What? Aspects of Identity in Nella Larsen's Novels." *Black American Literature Forum* 20 (1986): 97–111.

———. "Response to Kimberly W. Benston's 'Performing Blackness.'" In Baker and Redmond, *Afro-American Literary Study,* 185–89.

———, ed. *Changing Our Own Words.* New Brunswick: Rutgers University Press, 1989.

Wallace, Michelle. "Variations on Negation." In Gates, *Reading Black,* 52–67.

Washington, Mary Helen. "The Darkened Eye Restored: Notes toward a Literary History of Black Women." In *Invented Lives: Narratives of Black Women, 1860–1960,* xv–xxxi. Garden City, N.Y.: Anchor, 1987.

West, Cornel. "The New Cultural Politics of Difference." In Ferguson, *Out There,* 19–36.

———. *Race Matters.* New York: Vintage, 1994.

White, Walter. "The Paradox of Color." In Locke, *The New Negro,* 361–68.

Williams, Harry M., Jr. "When Black Is Right: The Life and Writings of George Schuyler." Ph.D. diss., Brown University, 1988.

Williamson, Joel. *New People.* New York: Free Press, 1980.

Wilson, William Julius. *The Declining Significance of Race.* Chicago: University of Chicago Press, 1978.

Wintz, Cary D. *Black Culture and the Harlem Renaissance.* Houston: Rice University Press, 1988.

Wright, Richard. *American Hunger.* 1944. New York: Harper and Row, 1977.

———. *Black Boy.* 1945. New York: Perennial Classics, 1966.

# Index

J. Martin Favor is an Assistant Professor of English at
Dartmouth College.

Library of Congress Cataloging-in-Publication Data
Favor, J. Martin.
Authentic Blackness : the folk in the new negro renaissance /
J. Martin Favor.
p.   cm.
Includes bibliographical references and index.
ISBN 0-8223-2311-7 (acid-free paper). — ISBN 0-8223-2345-1
(pbk. acid-free paper)
1. American literature—Afro-American authors—History
and criticism.   2. American literature—20th century—
History and criticism.   3. Harlem (New York, N.Y.)—
Intellectual life—20th century.   4. Afro-Americans in
literature.   5. Afro-Americans—Race identity.   6. Group
identity in literature.   7. Harlem Renaissance.   8. Race in
literature.   I. Title.
PS153.N5F38  1999
810.9′896073—dc21  98-51461  CIP

# DATE DUE

| APR 2 3 2003 | | | |
|---|---|---|---|
| | | | |
| | | | |
| | | | |
| | | | |
| | | | |
| | | | |
| | | | |
| | | | |
| | | | |
| | | | |
| | | | |
| | | | |
| | | | |
| | | | |
| | | | |
| | | | |